Just Work

JUST WORK

Russell Muirhead

HARVARD UNIVERSITY PRESS

Cambridge, Massachusetts, and London, England

First Harvard University Press paperback edition, 2007

Library of Congress Cataloging-in-Publication Data

Muirhead, Russell, 1965–
Just work / Russell Muirhead.
p. cm.
Includes bibliographical references and index.
ISBN-13 978-0-674-01558-6 (cloth: alk. paper)
ISBN-10 0-674-01558-4 (cloth: alk. paper)
ISBN-13 978-0-674-02408-3 (pbk.)
ISBN-10 0-674-02408-7 (pbk.)
1. Work—Philosophy. 2. Work—Psychological aspects.
3. Work—Social aspects. 4. Work ethic. I. Title.

HD4904.M75 2004
306.3′6—dc22   2004042211

Designed by Gwen Nefsky Frankfeldt

To Kate and Jim

Contents

Just Work

Introduction

"Do what you love—the money will follow." This advice, common enough, would have seemed strange and imprudent only two generations ago. The doctrine that we should be devoted to work is enduring and reflects a long association with the Protestant ethic. But the notion that we should be passionate about our work, or that if we follow our passions the rewards will take care of themselves, is something new. What would have been audacious fifty years ago is now a staple of career advice.[1] This contemporary advice embraces the aspiration and even the expectation of finding work that "fits" us in some important way. If the expectation is optimistic, still the aspiration to find work that fits our disposition and interests, our passions and purposes, points to an important standard that bears both on individual choices and on larger understandings of justice.

That we should avoid work to which we are ill suited, that we should not be miscast in one of our life's main activities or stuck serving purposes we cannot embrace, is of obvious importance. In this respect, the concept of fit addresses the basic question "Why is it right that *I* am doing *this?*" This is a personal question, though not a trivial one, as it reflects an understanding of both who we are and what we deserve. Its answer hinges on an understanding of how we might fit our work. In one sense, work is a good fit when it calls on the aptitudes and talents through which we can best contribute to society (or the market). When our abilities are aligned with the tasks or jobs society needs performed, work fits. This "social fit," between individual aptitudes and the tasks society generates, is necessary if people are to be moderately successful and societies efficient and productive.

But this is only part of what the idea of fit involves. Even when we are able to do our work well, we might still find that the work fails to engage our interests, purposes, and most distinctive capacities. To map our aptitudes onto social needs is one thing; to find work fulfilling is another. A "personal fit" with work, where work contributes to our own development and expression, may elude us even when we fit our work from a social perspective. The difficulty of combining social fit with personal fit reflects a provocative question at the heart of justice: Can we each get our due while at the same time contributing to the common good? When some do work that fits them badly yet contributes to socially important ends, another version of this question surfaces: Why ought some be constrained so that others or the whole may thrive? At the other extreme is an ideal of fit with work "where love and need are one."[2] According to this ideal, work is aligned with our purposes or good development; it engages us in the service of ends we endorse, expresses something of who we are, or develops our powers in ways we experience as good.

We often experience work as disconnected from such ideals as justice or freedom, and more like a necessity we would be better off without. In the face of the everyday difficulty of work, in defiance of the distractions we daily seek, we might say: just work! In this tone, the injunction to "just work" demands that we suspend doubt and dissatisfaction, and reconcile ourselves to what must be done, to the task at hand. At the same time, work demands too much and its connection to our identity is too profound to conceive of it only as the dictate of necessity, a strategy for survival. Richard Sennett, for instance, has illuminated the way work's predictability and the accumulation of skill offer—or, if they are absent, corrode—the basis for a unified identity over a lifetime.[3] For us, work is rarely *just* work in the diminutive sense of being *only* work. It is not something we can confine to a small and insignificant part of life. And (at least in America), we tend to take work seriously, too seriously to simply suspend deeper evaluation.

This raises important questions. What should we expect from work? Should the promise of work be restricted to its instrumental value—to the wages it brings? Is it right to invest work with the deeper promise of fulfillment? The answer to these questions depends not only on our taste and experience but also on the way we understand what it would mean for work to be fulfilling. This book argues, in short, that work is both fulfilling and just when it fits us.

Most of us face the unforgiving fact that "tomorrow is another working day."[4] Must the necessity of work be overcome to be truly free? Or is there some way of reconciling freedom and work? We could hold that work is consistent with freedom if we *choose* it. Freedom of occupational choice in a larger context that assures equal opportunity and nondiscrimination is a fundamental aspect of work's justice, but it does not stand alone. When we choose, we need other standards to guide our choice. With work, we often act from an understanding of what sort of work fits us, in both basic and profound ways: we choose well when we find fitting work. Fit reflects the constrained nature of choice; it recognizes that we cannot choose just as we might please, because we do not fit everything. Fit also involves an understanding of justice, as the following chapters show. Free choice and fit are thus two of the most fundamental regulative ideals that bear on the working life. If they sit alongside each other in some tension, each can also lend the other support. The ways in which the value of free choice invites considerations of fit, and that fit guides and constrains choice, is the central subject of Chapters 1 through 4.

Work and Necessity

One might think that neither choice nor fit matters terribly much, because work can seem so immune to the demands of any moral value or ideal. Work is often taken to be a necessary response to nature's stinginess, since its alternative for most is penury, insecurity, and dependence. To experience work as *necessary* seems to displace room for its moral evaluation: work is what it is and not what we might wish it to be. Perhaps the only truth about work's meaning is found in its necessity. Beyond this, work is endlessly differentiated. How could it be that the nineteenth-century domestic servant, the assembly-line worker, and the corporate consultant have anything in common? There are as many experiences of work as there are workers, as many kinds of work as there are jobs. Work cannot be hemmed in by natural definition or fixed like an element in the periodic table for, on the one hand, it reflects a historically contingent division of labor, while on the other, its every instance suggests the infinite expanse of the human mind and spirit. Even the drudgery of painting fences bends against the force of Tom Sawyer's imagination.[5] Work, it seems, has no single definition or essence, good or bad—only a history of various and unique experiences. It has no pure form.

Yet we know it when we do it, and thus can locate some rough definition that captures the "family resemblances" contained in the way we use the term.[6] At the head of this family is *pay*. We work to earn and spend.[7] Pay in turn reflects the fact that work answers needs and wants, either our own or another's. In this respect, work is about production and *contribution*. Yet even when it contributes, not all work pays, as every parent knows or as Robinson Crusoe's example attests. More to the point than pay is *effort*. Intellectually and physically, work is a strain, which is why the antonym of work is not only play, which takes effort, but also rest. Still, everything that requires effort is not work—writing a letter to a friend or swimming on a humid day take effort but hardly count as work. Along with pay and effort is something closer to the core: *compulsion.*

Compulsion may be explicit and violent, as in the Russian gulag, on the antebellum plantation, or, still, in the migrant farm labor of today's invisible fields.[8] Where brutal force is absent, work's compulsion may come from the insufficiency of nature or the psychic internalization of duty. What is universal about the experience of work is that it is not something we can forgo whenever we feel like it. Work might be done better or worse, with joy or with pain, from pride or from resignation, but it is done because it has to be done. A response to need and the demands of life, it is, as Bart Giamatti says, our "negotiation with death."[9] And the necessity of work extends beyond the need to survive. Our basic needs together with our habit of comparing ourselves with others nourish an infinite variety of wants. The psychology of ever-present desire, where as soon as one need or want is met "another uneasiness is ready to set us on work," means that work is a negotiation also with the desires that come into being when the prospect of death is not so immediate.[10] We may overcome the injustice of forced labor, we may steer ourselves from the margins to affluence, but we do not so easily escape work's discipline and constraint.

A fortunate few manage to meet the demands of necessity without feeling its pinch. Their work transcends compulsion and needs no spur. It is (or it seems on the outside) spontaneous and free. Yet spontaneous work too must provide a living. The background condition of even freely conscious labor is still a kind of need. Thus even those with desirable jobs, and those whose work seems on the outside like fun, often feel the underlying necessity of work. If not for all then for most, work is a command and not an option. It is done because we have to do it, because we are born and remain insufficient. The compulsion at the core of work gives the experience of work its distinctive taste. It is also what makes talking about the meaning and justice of work difficult. Lofty idealism overlooks the plain fact that when tomorrow must be another working day, speculation about the justice or moral meaning of work seems luxurious and irrelevant.[11]

Allied to this is the view that work is punishing and painful: "By its very nature," Studs Terkel writes, work is "about violence—to the spirit as well as to the body."[12] The enduring stain of original sin, work imposes painful discipline and stinging insult. The daily offenses of work are imposed by a miserly natural condition that never affords us enough and is full of hazard. At best, on this view, work's meaning is not found in the good things it cultivates, the understanding it conveys, or the freedom it expresses. Rather, work stands as an instrumental activity, good not for what it is but for what it brings. It is what we must do to make ourselves safe in the world and, if we are lucky and strong, also comfortable. Against the reality that we need to earn in order to spend, and to spend in order to live, the language of ideals and justice seem idle talk.

Work and Ideals

Fair enough: with work we are up against a hard matter that cannot be reshaped exactly according to our best arguments and deepest wishes. Yet necessity can be exaggerated, and claims about necessity can mask matters of social and political contingency. Work is not so necessary as sleep or gravity, for its necessity does not alone dictate its structure. The boundaries of necessity are themselves matters of dispute. In its particular arrangements work is not infinitely unyielding. The organization of tasks into specific job roles, the fact that some people do these jobs and others those, that some jobs are desirable and others miserable—these involve social arrangements that although difficult to transform are not matters of necessity. Work may be necessary, but our organization of it is not; as such, it invites evaluation and justification.

Nor is the assessment of work a new thing, a luxury enabled only by productivity and affluence; on the contrary, the assessment of work reflects the experience that even if work is necessary, this necessity need not be regrettable. Toil and pain do not define the whole experience of work. Even Terkel notes that some "find a savor in their daily job," and his interviews are compelling not because they depict people in pain but because they illustrate the connection between work and dignity.[13] The fantasy of escaping work is a humane and universal indulgence, but reflection suggests that even paradise would have its work. Adam works *before* the Fall at tilling and naming; Eden is no escape from the busy-ness of production and reproduction, of amending nature to suit human needs.[14] With the Fall the land was cursed, yet it was not poisoned or riddled with mines: the land might yet be fertile, and the occasion to work it experienced as a gift.[15]

Language, too, reflects the fact that pain and punishment are not the whole of work's meaning. As Hannah Arendt argues, *labor* reflects the hardship necessary for survival while *work* points more to efforts that issue in lasting achievement.[16] We speak, for instance, of the miner's labor and of Shakespeare's work—suggesting that work might bring accomplishment, praise, and pride. However, Arendt probably distinguishes too much. The pain of labor and the accomplishments of work are not so easily separated, and in English we use *work* to mean both. They sit beside each other and often are so deeply interwoven that one cannot be extricated from the other. Our language mirrors our experience: if work is about effort necessary to existence, sometimes so painful and constraining it feels like a punishment, it is also about effort we direct toward projects that are expressive, important, and satisfying.

The evaluation of work is not something foreign, an activity for experts who stand at a distance. Rather, it arises from the experience of work itself, with the dueling possibilities it contains. The experience of work as pleasant and unpleasant, useful and destructive, prompts deeper reflection about the meaning and justice of work. That we choose our work only lends additional pressure to the matter. The experience of work thus invites us to construct a "meaningful" or "legitimate" account, a framework that makes sense of the demands and rewards the working life contains. Many try, if only on occasion, to conceive their work in "an interpretative context that gives it meaning."[17]

In "giving an account" of work, we explain it and situate it with reference to larger aims and values we embrace. We relate the pain and accomplishment of work to other commitments and ideals about the kinds of people we would like to be, the kind of place we would like to be a part of, and the sort of life we take ourselves to deserve. To experience work as meaningful is to be able to give an account that makes sense of our work in this broader context. The account we generate may or may not reflect well on work but in either case is distinguished from resignation to work's necessity. When we give an account of an activity like work, we invoke not only personal preferences ("I like working outside") but also "regulative ideals." These are public in that they reside in and are carried by the larger culture. While they are not always connected with formal politics, they may on occasion motivate certain kinds of legislation.

One powerful regulative ideal is that of "meaningful" or "fulfilling" work. As an ideal that often determines individual choices about jobs and careers, it also may inform both evaluations of work and the design of jobs. It is a greedy ideal: it demands much, at times too much—and as such might be responsible for significant disappointment. Yet it is one that must be taken seriously, not only because of work's essential place in a democratic culture but also because it reflects a longing both noble and democratic to invest quotidian life with heartfelt commitment and joy. Such a longing resists the weight of necessity; it reflects that part of the human spirit that affirms its dignity. This book attempts to take the promise of fulfilling work seriously by examining what it entails with rigor and sympathy.

Freedom and Fit

At least two broad ideals bear directly on the evaluation of work: freedom and fit. On one hand, the value of freedom suggests that work is just if we freely choose it. On the other, we take work to give us what we deserve insofar as it is fitting, in some important respect. There is a clear tension between the two. In their most narrow and extreme forms, the two values stand forthrightly opposed, their opposition stemming from foundational differences about the meaning of justice. Yet the argument of the first four chapters holds that neither value wholly precludes the other. A free society, such as ours, will be one in which fitting roles matter intensely; and fitting work itself will both depend on and support conditions of freedom.

If we were to take the value of freedom to an extreme, as Chapter 1 shows, we would need to somehow overcome every tincture of work's necessity. Fully free, we would be able not only to freely accept work but also, therefore, to reject it. Work would be merely an option, a lifestyle choice: every vocation an avocation. Yet freedom as we experience it is not only a utopian ideal but also a concrete political achievement. It depends on a certain kind of politics—a liberal political regime—which, if it maintains freedom, also asks certain things of its citizens. One of its requirements is work. As work is something even a free people cannot avoid, the matter of how we fit our work is correspondingly inescapable. Indeed, the experience of work today amplifies the importance of fitting work, as Chapter 2 demonstrates.

The ideal of fitting work nonetheless evokes suspicion, especially when taken as a moral and political ideal. The notion that persons are fitted to particular roles has long been allied with an aristocratic understanding of justice, which denies equal opportunity and free choice in the name of restricting people to their proper places. Most famously, Aristotle argued that even slavery is just for those who fit the role—the natural slaves. Chapter 3 turns directly to these ancient arguments about fit to show that the underlying concept of fit, which even in Aristotle affirms that individuals deserve roles that develop their best capacities, more effectively criticizes than cements social hierarchy.

The notion that every person has a claim to develop his or her capacities confirms the democratic intuition that each equally has a life to live, that no one was made for another's use. This democratic understanding of fit thus puts a special burden on work that threatens to overwhelm or negate an individual's claims. The burden is particularly evident in service work, especially the sort of domestic service in which one subsumes one's own needs for the sake of tending to the personal needs of others. Domestic service, as Chapter 4 demonstrates, has never meshed with democratic self-understandings. The example of domestic service points to a more general minimal standard fit, which asks that work be bounded or contained even when it is consented to, such that it permits those who do it to live a life that is in some sense their own.

From the Work Ethic to an Ethic of Work

A job is sometimes just a job. Discrete tasks truncated from other parts of life, jobs are done for the sake of something outside them, like meeting the demands of self-support or shouldering familial responsibilities—in short, for the money. At the extreme, jobs are like "gigs," disconnected from the larger flow of one's life, akin to a musician's one-night engagement at the airport lounge. Often the only way to ensure that jobs satisfy the standard of fit is to bound them, so that they neither so exhaust our energies nor consume our time as to leave nothing for the rest of life. Limited in this way, they enable us to engage our most authentic energies and pursue our most important purposes *outside* of work.

Yet many hope for a more ideal kind of fit, where work is not only a job but a career, even a calling. Chapters 5 through 8 look to the possibility of a more complete kind of fit, where work itself is a source of fulfillment and devotion. An ideal of fitting work—suggested by the Protestant doctrine of the calling—is at the core of the work ethic, which as Weber wrote at the start of the twentieth century, still "prowls about in our lives like the ghost of dead religious beliefs."[18] Chapter 5 shows how the Protestant ethic established work itself as worthy of devotion. Yet the ethic also contained an inner fragility, the seeds of its own unmaking. It failed to locate anything in the activity of work itself connected to the transcendental purposes work was meant to express, thereby placing an enormous burden on faith. When faith wavers, devotion to a calling relies more on the sheer force of individual will than on goods discerned through the activity of working. In this way, the Protestant work ethic threatens to give way to a mere ethic of work—a habit and a discipline, disjoined from the transcendental purposes that the work ethic is meant to reflect.

If the theological convictions that originally supported the Protestant calling have diminished, the aspiration to find a calling has not. Characterized less by religious duty than by passion and enthusiasm, the contemporary understanding of callings is cast more in terms of fulfillment in this life than salvation in the next. Chapter 6 turns to John Stuart Mill, who placed the promise of fulfillment at the center of his liberalism. If alluring, fulfillment is not an easy achievement, and Mill's account leaves ample room for doubt that its promise can be democratized. Yet later, popular writers like Betty Friedan, the subject of Chapter 7, would do exactly this. Friedan generalizes the promise of fulfillment and also maps it directly onto the working life. The problem with restricting women to a domestic role, for Friedan, is not simply that it is unjustly coercive but that the domestic role is also unfulfilling—indeed, on her terms, it is unfit for anyone of average competence. Better, she argues, to pursue not only a job but a fitting career that affords the chance for real social contribution, self-development, and self-expression. The good things of life are found in fitting work, from which no one should be excluded. In broadcasting the promise of fulfillment, Friedan in her own secular way follows a strain of the older Protestant ethic: she believes that every person could have a career and every career could be a calling. She also inherits the frailty of that ethic, for she can generalize the promise of fulfilling careers only at the cost of ignoring the reality of most work. Any specific account of the specific goods to be found in the actual activity of work eludes Friedan.

Such an account would need to carefully attend to the kinds of "internal goods" careers might offer. Internal goods, as Chapter 8 explains, are inextricably linked to an activity. In this way, they are distinct from goods (like money) that one might gain any number of ways and that are therefore only contingently connected to the activities that garner them. These internal goods offer a way of understanding how we might fit our work such that we experience it as fulfilling, as being itself worthy of our energy and devotion. The passion that we today associate with callings, or with work that fits in an ideal way, finds its reason and its grounding in the internal goods that work might, at its best, offer.

We tend to love both what is ours and what is good, and often indulge the tendency to think that what is ours is *also* good. The working life is undoubtedly *our* life, and so it will remain. Equally certain is that it can be improved, and the Conclusion will consider various ways it can be reformed with a view to fitting work. As Chapter 8 and the Conclusion show, work's claim is at best a qualified one, and an understanding of fitting work bids that as we endeavor to improve it, we also keep it in its place.

Democracy and the Value of Work

1

Once at the center of political and social theory, work now stands at the margins. Work shapes workers, and not only for the better: this was obvious to classic defenders as well as critics of commercial society. Adam Smith, who sought to unveil and defend the motives and policies that render nations productive and wealthy, appreciated the formative effects of an increasingly specialized division of labor. On one hand, Smith noticed the way work concentrates the mind, spurring discoveries and inventions that in turn contribute to more efficient production (this was an observation later shared by Abraham Lincoln, in the defense of "free labor" he mounted against advocates of slavery). On the other, he saw too that an elaborate division of labor creates jobs so simple they render those who do them "as stupid and ignorant as it is possible for an individual to become."[1] Seventy-five years later the most potent critic of commercial society, Karl Marx, founded his moral criticism of capitalism on an analysis of the connection between our work and our identity. Work is never only an instrumental activity, something we do to sustain life; instead it both expresses and forms who we are: "What individuals are," he says, "depends on the material conditions of their production."[2]

Nor is the kind of attention that thinkers like Smith and Marx gave to the character of work anomalous. The most influential of contemporary liberal political theorists, John Rawls, also asserts that economic systems are not to be evaluated only for their instrumental value in satisfying needs and wants. "How men work together now to satisfy their present desires," he says, "affects the desires they will have later on, the kinds of persons they will be . . . Since economic arrangements have these effects, and indeed must do so, the choice of these institutions involves some view of human good and the design of institutions to realize it."[3] This is a reminder that freedom of occupational choice, equality of opportunity, and a fair distribution of resources do not exhaust the categories of evaluation that liberals might bring to the world of work. Even in a society where rights are protected and distributions are fair, work is not a good we might choose like every other. The structure of work, or the "economic system," is a precondition of individual choice, and molds as it also constrains and directs that choice. The achievement of a just society that secures the bases of self-respect and protects individual rights does not displace the classic concern with work as a formative activity.

Yet contemporary political theory has had more to say about pluralism, toleration, virtue, equality of opportunity, and rights than it has about the character of work. Why? No explanation can ignore the historical failure of Marxism. The totalitarian expression of Marxism in the twentieth century suggests that any politicized concern with human fulfillment is bound to collapse in practice into tyrannical state regulation over the whole of life. Where Marx imagined that political revolution could create conditions that repair the human condition and "return man to himself," liberals accept that alienation is an inevitable part of human life and that no existing social world can contain the fullness of human possibility.[4] Thus the Marxist concern with work's fulfilling or alienating possibilities is often left to subjects like sociology and psychology, which attend to the meanings experienced in social as opposed to political life.[5] The problem of meaningful work also falls to management experts, whose concern lies less with moral and political life and more with attitudes conducive to efficiency, profit, and good corporate morale.[6]

Freedom and the Obligation to Work

What contemporary political theory does have to say about work centers on the core values of freedom and equality. The principle of equality insists on nondiscrimination in the distribution of jobs. Careers should be open to talents, and each person should find a fair equality of opportunity to develop his or her talents and to compete for jobs. How the principle of freedom applies to work is a trickier matter. At least, it demands that people have the right to quit and to change jobs as they please, and forbids all forms of physical coercion. But in a deeper sense, to be free is to have the opportunity to live a life expressive of a plan that in some sense can be understood as our own.[7] Yet in spite of the Herculean power over nature with which modern science and technology have endowed us, nature remains a formidable obstacle to human freedom. If they rival the wonders of nature, the wonders of technology have not overcome the necessity of work. We might choose a career, if we are lucky; but it is rare that one can choose whether to work at all.

In the eyes of some, the necessity of work is not so much a natural fact but a social injustice. According to Phillippe Van Parijs, a just society would maximize the "real freedom to choose among the various lives one might wish to lead," which in turn would require that individuals not be forced to work from material need. Real freedom thus depends on the state's guaranteeing a minimum income of the "highest sustainable level" to all citizens. In contrast to other types of welfare provision, a guaranteed income is also, in his view, the most effective way of improving the lot of the least fortunate.[8] Central to Van Parijs's argument is the view that jobs should be seen as scarce assets that some (namely, workers) co-opt to the exclusion of nonworkers. Jobs are more scarce than they would be in a perfect labor market for a couple of reasons: because higher wages can stimulate productivity and because employers wish to avoid the costs of rehiring and retraining, employers often pay higher wages than the labor market would dictate. Thus there are many who are willing (and able) to do jobs for lower wages than the persons who now do them. The difference between what the wage workers actually receive and the market-clearing wage (the wage at which there is no one willing to accept the job for less) is the "employment rent," or surplus wage. This surplus wage means that labor markets generate more involuntary unemployment than they would if they operated with perfect efficiency. Van Parijs holds that these economic rents not only should be shared by those who have a preference for (and are fortunate enough to find) paying work, but also should be distributed more generally in the form of a guaranteed income to those who do not work for pay (and thus monopolize scarce jobs), even if it is because they are simply unwilling to work.

The main point of a universal basic income is that it would make freedom not merely an ideal or a formal legal condition but a *real* condition available to all. Were we frugal enough to live on the guaranteed income alone, we could choose to concentrate our waking hours on the unpaid work so essential to households: raising children, for instance, or looking after the sick and elderly. Or we might devote ourselves to more leisurely activities like playing poker, surfing, or writing love letters. Whatever, a universal basic income would give us the *real* freedom to choose for ourselves, without the painful intrusion of work. This scheme would also promise to ameliorate the problem of bad or unfitting work: absent the raw necessity that compels people to accept monotonous, exhausting, or dirty jobs at low wages, employers would have to either pay more or improve the intrinsic attractions of work, or both.

Yet this policy is also likely to cause deep resentment—of a morally understandable and defensible sort—among workers. The root of the problem is that the universal basic income would not be entirely funded through common assets that fell, as it were, into the community's lap—as shares of revenues from Alaskan oil are distributed to citizens of that state. The basic income would also be funded through the work other people do. And why should those who are unwilling to work in the first place get to live off the labor of others? For Van Parijs, the willingness to work is simply a taste, and a really free society would equip all to pursue their tastes while not biasing some over others. The taste for work, in his view, is akin to the taste for attending the opera or major league baseball games: first, one's attendance reduces the supply of seats available to others; second, one's preference for work is an individual matter that a just government would neither endorse nor impede. But few people regard the willingness to work as a mere preference, and few if any regard jobs as simply scarce assets akin to seats in a stadium. Even desirable work takes discipline. The same job that offers enjoyment in some moments will have to be endured in others, and the willingness to work is more often an expression of personal responsibility and social obligation than it is a lifestyle preference. For these reasons, any sizable universal basic income "would fail," as Jon Elster says, "because it would be perceived as unfair, indeed as exploitative."[9]

The perception that a guaranteed income would be exploitative rests on the argument that it violates social reciprocity, or the idea that all who choose to benefit from a system of social cooperation should also, insofar as they are able, "do their bit" to contribute to the creation of those benefits. Redistributing from workers to those unwilling to work establishes a parasitic relationship in which the unwilling exploit a resource (jobs) they do not want in the first place, to their own advantage.[10] For the voluntarily unemployed to command part of the wages workers earn because they might have wanted to compete for those jobs (had they more of a taste for work) is a form of usurpation. It is on par with standing in line at the post office—with nothing to mail—only so you can sell your place once you get to the front of the line, or to buying up Web domains (like www.famouscompany.edu) you have no use for only for the purpose of later selling them to legitimate users, or occupying unsettled land you have no intention of improving, for the purpose of making a profit by later selling it to those who would use it.[11]

In line with the intuition that a guaranteed income would be parasitic or exploitative, Rawls insists that citizens do not have a right to use public transfers to finance a preference for leisure: "Those who surf all day off Malibu must find a way to support themselves and would not be entitled to public funds."[12] No one, in Rawls's view, has a right to a leisured life that is funded by fellow citizens. "We are not to gain from others," Rawls says, "without doing our fair share."[13] And the willingness to work is central to reciprocity, or "doing our fair share": working, as Amy Gutmann and Dennis Thompson argue, "shows that you are carrying your share of the social burden."[14]

Aside from the parasitic aspects of a guaranteed income, just liberal democracies require a measure of abundance, which in turn requires work. In the most general sense, economic growth and the corollary promise that all can be better off simultaneously make inequality palatable in fact and justifiable in theory. What matters most for conservatives is that everyone benefits in some way from growth, however much growth aggravates inequality. For egalitarian liberals, inequality is justifiable only when it maximally benefits those on the bottom. But for both, productivity and growth allow politics to escape the ancient condition where one's gain is another's loss, a condition that nourishes incessant conflict, breeds ascriptive and aristocratic ideologies, and invites the few to oppress the rest. A growth economy gives the strong, the weak, and those in between a stake in the regime, since all can improve their situations together.

For this reason many take work to be not only a necessary thing but also a kind of social obligation. Just democracies cannot be neutral, as Gutmann and Thompson argue, "between ways of life that contribute to economic productivity and those that do not."[15] To say that the state cannot be wholly unbiased between productive and unproductive ways of life does not mean, in their view, that it should coerce people to be productive by legally enforcing an obligation to work. Gutmann and Thompson look instead to the softer sanction of public opinion and the gentler prod of tax legislation (specifically an inheritance tax) to motivate productive activity. Noting that the obligation to work applies not only to the poor but also to "those at the top," they say: "Those who choose to live off inherited wealth without contributing their own labor to society may deserve no more respect from their fellow citizens than the Malibu surfers."[16] This "respect" is conferred not by the state but by public opinion; it is expressed not by law but in the way we regard one another.

These considerations are not sufficient to reject a universal basic income in any form—it might be revised in such a way as to account for the importance of reciprocity and diminish its exploitative aspect.[17] But the concern about reciprocity reminds us that even a universal basic income would not literally do away with the necessity of work: some will have to work if others are to collect a basic income. Moreover, it is not at all certain that a universal basic income would solve the problem of undesirable or unpleasant work in one efficient stroke. A guaranteed income could have the large-scale effect, as Stuart White mentions, of depressing the incentives to work and develop one's skills. In this event, employers might respond by creating low-skill jobs that are relatively easy to fill, thus deteriorating the quality of work.[18] This is not to say that some version of a guaranteed income would not be the most effective way of securing a basic complement of real freedom on a relatively equal basis across a whole society; indeed it might be the best available policy with respect to those goals. But it would neither eradicate the necessity of work nor displace the general question of bad or low-quality work. Even with a universal guaranteed income, work will be a fact of life for most citizens in liberal democracies, and the quality of work will remain a matter deserving of careful attention.

Whatever else we are, as democrats we are a working people. We see this in our beliefs, such as the work ethic; in our self-understandings, which cause us to identify with our work; in our policies, which encourage and even compel work; in our behavior, for we work a lot, often beyond the dictate of need; and in our values, which ally the working life with human dignity. This affirmation of the working life has its coercive side, but it also reflects in a democratic culture a kind of equality or shared condition that tempers even when it does not eliminate differences in income, wealth, power, and ability. Any democratic culture must in some way affirm the value of work. The aristocratic disdain for work carried with it not only an affirmation of leisure but also a disdain for workers, who were thought too debilitated by the discipline of work to deliberate well or function as full citizens.[19] The democratic faith, by contrast, is that work supports and expresses our dignity. But if this is to be more than a staple of dogma, one needs to inquire seriously into the promise and problems of the working life.

The values of democratic culture thus invite us to take seriously the promise and the problems of work. This leads to a number of questions about the meaning and justice of work: Do people have a right to work?[20] What justifies differentials in pay? In addition to questions about the right to work and fair pay are others that address the quality of work: How do we justify the fact that some have good jobs while others do grueling, repetitive, and dirty work? What does work need to be like for a work ethic to be commendable? Among these questions, contemporary political theorists have focused less on the quality of work, or the society's distribution of good and bad work.[21]

The aversion to assessing the distribution of good and bad work comes in part from a respect for freedom and the diversity of individual tastes: what counts as good is for each to decide. Different people will bring different preferences to the workplace. Some will prefer stimulating work, others routine; some will prefer the camaraderie of the workplace, others like focused solitude; some will prefer a challenge, others security; some will prefer meaningful work to which they can be devoted, others ironic distance from work.[22] Any narrow argument that claims government policy should guarantee meaningful work will fail to respect this diversity, as it will also fail to respect the freedom of each to generate and act on his or her own orientation to work.

Regulative Ideals: Meaningful Work

The ideal of meaningful work, like regulative ideals more generally, seems to invite a kind of perfectionist politics that by legislating comprehensive ideals thereby undermines respect for individuals' right to live by ideals of their own. Against this perceived perfectionist threat, the most stringent liberal view seeks to exclude ideals from political life. Embracing a principle of neutrality instead of perfectionism, this view holds that political decisions should be independent of any larger conception of what "gives value to life." Regulative ideals should rely for their force on the voluntary assent of individuals, while the state, for its part, is neutral with respect to various and rival conceptions of the good life.[23] Meaningful work, on this view, is a matter for voluntary associations and individuals themselves—not politics.

Allied to this is a view about the difference between the reasons we may use in political life and those we invoke in our personal lives. "Not all reasons," Rawls says, "are public reasons." The idea of public reason, as developed by Rawls and others, insists that we are required to offer reasons that acknowledge other citizens as free and equal, at least when offering reasons that concern matters of fundamental justice and constitutional essentials.[24] What it means for a reason to acknowledge others as free and equal is a subtle philosophic matter, but the idea of what is ruled out by public reason and what counts as a public reason is often intuitive enough. For instance, reasons drawn from religious conceptions of life or comprehensive moral philosophies about how we should live cannot serve as public reasons because they would fail to respect the freedom of citizens to affirm or reject such ideas for themselves. While Rawls, as we will see, advocates a view of public reason that allows regulative ideals to exercise great force in political life, others, with a more narrow conception of the sorts of arguments that can qualify as public reason, argue for excluding such ideals from political life.

Consider, for instance, how this stringent view bears on regulative ideals such as the value of artistic expression. Some will hold an ideal of artistic appreciation and expression as an integral part of a life well lived; they will esteem individuals who cultivate artistic taste, while also admiring societies for the music, dance, painting, or performance their members produce. Yet an appreciation of art's place in a good life would not warrant public funding of the arts, on this view. The problem is not simply that an appreciation of fine arts might belong only to an elite minority but that it is illicit for a liberal state to uphold artistic practices as part of an intrinsically good way of life—even if that appreciation is held by a large majority. Regardless of the numbers who endorse funding the arts, to *justify* such a policy by reference to the place of art in a good life or by reference to the intrinsic value of art would uphold one ideal of life above others, and would fail to respect the freedom of each to choose and act from his own conception of the good. Thus, on this view, a legislator who follows the constraints of public reason, it seems, cannot say, "Art is an expression of our common culture and individual genius; at its best it is an expression of human excellence and thus deserves public support." Legislators can, however, argue that art needs public support because collective action problems undercut private support of the arts, or that the state has a duty to maintain a range of cultural options from which individuals can choose.[25]

Yet the argument for entirely screening out regulative ideals from political life is noticeably strained. In the case of art funding, restricting our reasons to the necessity of overcoming market failures and the end of maintaining the richness of a culture would likely compel legislators to misrepresent simultaneously their own motives and those of their constituents. It is reasonable to assume that legislators who support public funding of the arts may be motivated by some regard for the moral value and cultural importance of artistic expression and experience. Were this not so, they probably wouldn't care much about the problems of assurance and isolation that afflict arts funding. Yet were such legislators to offer reasons that square with the strict interpretation of liberal neutrality, they would misrepresent what really motivates them. It would be more honest, possibly more effective, and more attuned to the persuasive and representative tasks of a legislature to admit this sort of regulative ideal more directly into legislative deliberation.[26]

The strict separation of public and nonpublic reasons is overdrawn, and a more latitudinarian interpretation of the boundaries of public reason, such as the one Rawls has defended in his more recent work, would allow for the more honest and straightforward invocation of regulative ideals in public life. In this more permissive interpretation, the strictures of public reason apply most forcefully only when constitutional essentials (like basic individual rights) and questions of fundamental justice arise. Public reason therefore applies with particular gravity to the Constitution and its interpretation, and it is the Supreme Court—rather than the public forum more generally—that stands as the "exemplar of public reason." Since "many if not most political questions do not concern those fundamental matters," the constraints of public reason will not apply to many issues.[27] The demands of public reason also apply selectively: they bind officeholders, candidates, and citizens when they vote or advocate in the public political forum *and* when matters of fundamental justice are at stake. Even then, public reason applies in a looser and more forgiving way in the public political forum than it does in constitutional jurisprudence. It is permissible, for instance, for citizens and legislators to invoke comprehensive doctrines to support policies or principles, so long as "in due course" they offer corroborating "properly public reasons" for the same policies and principles.[28]

In this more permissive interpretation of public reason, Rawls recognizes that comprehensive doctrines are often the source of the reasons that motivate us most vitally in politics and elsewhere. It is because we think art has a place in a life well lived that we argue for public funding of art, or because we think that labor is potentially expressive of our fundamental personality that we care about meaningful work. He also acknowledges that most political issues (here we might include issues such as funding the arts or improving the quality of work) do not involve constitutional essentials in such a way that the reasons we bring to discussing them need to fully conform to the most strict understanding of public reason. Ideals such as the intrinsic value of art, the importance of wilderness preservation, or meaningful work are thus at home in the public forum. There need not be a wall of separation between the background culture that supports a range of comprehensive conceptions of the good and the policies and principles we advocate in the political sphere.

In this respect, the permissive interpretation of public reason has an affinity with "moderate perfectionism," which also seeks to admit moral, philosophic, and religious ideals to public deliberation but which rejects the sort of extreme perfectionism that would have governments "pursue all moral considerations at all costs."[29] As Rawls recognizes that "many if not most" political issues do not involve constitutional essentials like basic rights, so the moderate perfectionists point out that not all of what governments do is coercive nor is it all coercive in the same degree.[30] While the strictures of public reason apply when we justify to each other the use of government's coercive power, it is unrealistic and unduly restrictive to suppose that every piece of legislation reflects the full coercive power of the state. While all taxation is coercive, some things that taxes are used for are more coercive than others. A large category of laws encourage or facilitate rather than compel: it is one thing to build parks, another to compel people to play soccer; one thing to fund museums, another to force people to attend exhibits; one thing to encourage developers to preserve green space, another to relocate neighborhoods and rebuild according to a planner's ideal. This category of legislation, which does not directly coerce individuals, may be informed by broad regulative ideals without violating the constitutionally essential rights that protect individual liberties. A regulative ideal of meaningful work (along with regulative ideals of other sorts), while of obvious personal import, can also be politically relevant in this way: it might inform legislation that facilitates and encourages even when it does not directly compel.

We are not faced with a stark choice between an extreme perfectionism that legislates in the name of ideals but undermines freedom, on one hand, and an extreme version of liberal neutrality that excludes public consideration of all regulative ideals for the sake of respecting freedom, on the other. Politics in the largest sense can admit of (and respond to) regulative ideals while suitably securing basic liberties. There is a great deal of public space between the sort of coercive legislation that demands careful public justification and the background culture or civil society that nourishes a variety of comprehensive conceptions of the good life. Regulative ideals operate at this middle level: they have a wider public function than merely private preferences, but they do not go as deep as foundational principles of justice.[31] Given the central importance of work in liberal democracy, one would expect regulative ideals of meaningful work to play a powerful role in society. It is one thing to hold that we should not use the coercive power of the state to impose some narrow conception of meaningful work on everyone, but it would be unwarranted to conclude that therefore the question of meaningful work should be an entirely private or personal matter. Even those who argue against legally enforcing meaningful work affirm that it can serve as a "regulative ideal" that "any decent political economy," we should hope, will gradually fulfill.[32]

Neither the broad interpretation of public reason nor moderate perfectionism is a license for legislators to invoke every prejudice they or their constituents might hold, and sometimes the force of regulative ideals will best be left to society rather than legislation.

For example, turning again to Gutmann and Thompson's argument for the obligation to work, we can see that they affirm the value of work as a social obligation without insisting that it be legally enforced. They do not claim that those who are able yet unwilling to work should be jailed; nor do they claim that the society's interest in productivity warrants inducing those who produce less than they could (perhaps they work part-time because they enjoy spending the rest of their time reading novels or talking with friends) to maximize their productivity. Rather, they rely on softer social sanctions of shame and admiration (the "respect of one's fellow citizens") and laws that encourage but do not compel (an inheritance tax) to endorse *some* productivity over none. They invoke the obligation to work as a regulative ideal that might inform public policy, not one that would be enforced by the crudest legal means.

Politics and the Democratic Condition

To accept meaningful work as a politically relevant regulative ideal does not issue in new justifications for using the state's coercive power. But politics is never only about the state's monopoly on violence. In the broadest sense, even liberal politics concerns not just the restriction of governmental power but also the social, economic, and cultural conditions that give individual freedom its particular context. Politics in the largest sense is about the lives individuals can choose under particular conditions, and the lives they are impelled to live or even choose in a particular society and regime. These lives are composed of roles: parent, spouse, worker, to name a few. It matters that we choose these roles for ourselves. But the choices we make run only so deep, for the roles themselves exist independent of our choice. They come to us on a limited menu, one that is carried by social conventions and beliefs that in turn are sustained and buttressed by families, voluntary associations, traditions, and laws. From the perspective of consent, what matters most is that these roles are open to all, that no one is either forced into them or excluded from them. Thus we need to ensure that people have the freedom to choose among roles and to exit, when they wish, those they have assumed. But this does not exhaust the questions we ought to ask about such roles, even from a concern with justice. We ought to inquire, too, about the conditions of choice, the sorts of choices individuals are impelled to make under constraints, as well as the quality and variety of the options available for people to choose from.

This is especially so when it comes to work. As a descriptive matter and (if we reject a guaranteed minimum income as parasitic) as a normative matter, the working life is something that citizens necessarily share. The working life is *our* life. As we have seen, the necessity or obligatory character of work is in tension with the liberal ideal that citizens should be free (not only formally but effectively) to form and act from their own conception of the good. Yet work is one of the most common and inescapable constraints on our freedom. This raises a crucial question: can the regulative ideals that concern work be modeled entirely on the liberal values of freedom and equality? Or will they at times follow a different cue, one that more fully recognizes the reality that work itself is a kind of restraint, a sort of discipline?

Any full account of the justice of work would certainly need somehow to reconcile the work people do (and at some level *have* to do) with their freedom. It would take stock of how work might look if its form resulted solely from our choices. Yet since work as it appears in the world will reflect not only our freedom but also our need, since it does not and probably cannot reflect our choices precisely, it remains something to which we often need to attune or accommodate or even reconcile ourselves. The ideal of fitting work recognizes the constrained character of freedom. It acknowledges our freedom, since fitting work is work we might more likely endorse.[33] At the same time, the concept of fit acknowledges that freedom in the world of work is always circumscribed. The category of fit thus allows for the possibility that even when work is good, it is something we have to make our peace with.

The ideal of fitting work also acknowledges the special kind of relationship that work involves. Along with family and religion, work remains one of the central activities constituting everyday life. Work is instrumental (we work to earn and spend), but is rarely only that: it is also formative. Devoting the bulk of our waking hours to a particular activity over many years has an effect on who we are, whether we like it or not. In a limited but crucial way, we are what we do ("What do you do?" is a kind of shorthand for "Who are you?"). In one sense, this reflects the way work positions us in a kind of hierarchy—both in the hierarchy of authority within organizations and in the larger social hierarchy represented by differences in income and wealth. If it is often inexplicit, it is no secret that some jobs are admired for their authority, command, glamour, compensation—in short, their prestige. And others are scorned. Our work makes manifest where we fall—or where we have climbed—in the social hierarchy. Yet we are also what we do in a more constitutive sense. What we do all day habituates and orients us in profound ways that over time impress a pattern on our emotional and intellectual life. Work might make us more compassionate or more stern, more decisive or more resentful, more deft or more argumentative. The way we spend the bulk of our waking energy can even come to inform our larger posture toward the world, depending on whether work prods us to experience the world as hostile or alien, compliant or beneficent. This is why for many work cannot be merely another of life's routines but is rather a key source of their identity.[34]

The aspiration to work that fits us, as both individuals and as human beings, is one I locate in the public culture of American life, in the way many evaluate work. This aspiration, widely if not universally shared, in turn points to an ancient understanding of justice, where justice addresses what we as individuals morally deserve, and what we deserve depends on what fits us. Because it focuses on what we deserve, the justice of fit is distinct from Rawls's justice as fairness, which concerns what we would accept under impartial conditions. Yet if they are in tension with each other, they are not quite face-to-face rivals because they apply at different levels. Justice as fairness most directly addresses constitutional essentials, while the justice of fit concerns "middle level" regulative ideals that operate in civil society. Each might influence legislation, though in different ways. Justice as fairness, in its way, addresses legislation from above by offering a model of impartiality that legislators can follow when basic principles of justice are at stake. It is most relevant when legislation is directly and obviously coercive. Regulative ideals like justice as fit influence legislation from below, when legislators represent and advance the sort of ethical notions that their constituents endorse. It is most relevant when legislation addresses not constitutional essentials but the circumstances of everyday life.

The regulative ideal of fit reflects the aspirations people bring to the world of work, as it also elucidates the common opinion that work somehow supports human dignity. What would be required of us to fit our work? What would be required of work? What is the difference between a good fit and a bad one? Are there some useful jobs that cannot be said to fit anyone very well? And if so, how should these be allocated? This book will engage these questions and others in a way that will be at times uncomfortable, for I do not presuppose that the familiar terms of equal opportunity and free choice exhaust the categories with which we might evaluate the world of work. Yet uncomfortable categories are necessary if we are to understand the sources of pride and disappointment (and the sense of dignity and justice) that our way of life contains.

2

Fitting Work in the Contemporary Economy

Regulative ideals are never simply imposed by social critics or intellectuals. If they have a hold on people, it is because they are rooted in common experience. As I argued in the Introduction, ideals of work grow out of its experience; philosophic reflection may clarify or assess such ideals, but it does not establish them. An ideal of fitting work is embedded in the contemporary experience of work, at least in America, as this chapter will show. It is underscored by recent developments, such as the very immediate relationship individuals have to market risks, and by more general and enduring attitudes, such as the affirmation of the working life. Consent, too, is not only a theoretical standard but a regulative ideal of popular force. We care, quite sensibly, that we have the right to accept or reject work as we please, without any change in our public standing as citizens. Yet consent, as the first part of this chapter shows, does not displace a concern with fitting work. On the contrary, the fact that we choose our work makes understanding how we might best fit our work more urgent.

Consent as a Regulative Ideal

One might hold that consent is itself sufficiently powerful to address the question of meaningful work, and that no auxiliary regulative ideal of meaningful work need be entertained. Adequately institutionalizing the norm of free consent, in this view, would fully address questions about the quality of work. This argument in its strongest form looks beyond the kind of consent that occurs in everyday life—exhibited, for instance, when we take or refuse a job. This sort of everyday consent is important, of course, because it is practical: it can be signified, recorded, and enforced. Chains and guns are enough to show that the slave does not consent. Practical and important though it is, actual consent does not fully satisfy the interest in respecting individual freedom, because consent as it actually occurs is too often marred by inequalities of knowledge, power, and social standing. As it actually appears in the world, consent is never perfectly free. This is why the more sophisticated theories of justice that give a prominent place to consent, such as Rawls's *Theory of Justice,* look not to the actual consent individuals offer in real-life situations but to the more perfect consent that anyone might give in a (hypothetical) situation of true equality. Only when the basic structure of society embodies principles that we would choose under such an ideal contractual situation, Rawls argues, do individual acts of consent acquire their full moral value. What counts for the justice of work is not the actual consent we give when we take a job but the consent we *would* give under ideal circumstances to the social structure and the larger social mechanisms of allocating jobs.

As a happy by-product, this free consent to the principles governing the basic structure of society might address the matter of meaningful work. In a truly just society, bad work might disappear or at least be ameliorated, since the more equal distribution of resources such a society would exhibit would make it less likely that people would agree to a job out of sheer need (this, as we have seen, is one reason Van Parijs supports a guaranteed minimum income). In a just society, hard work would be softened by the fact that the least advantaged would possess more bargaining power. Rawls himself tends to this view: in a society regulated by freely chosen principles of justice, he suggests, "no one need be servilely dependent on others and made to choose between monotonous and routine occupations which are deadening to human thought and sensibility."[1]

Yet there is reason to think that this happy picture, in which a just society founded on ideal consent brings meaningful work for all, is utopian. In some cases, no amount of fiddling with the conditions of work makes the work more interesting, elevating, challenging, or varied. The wars that sometimes need to be fought, the messes cleaned, the fuel mined, the food picked—all point to the likelihood that some work will be endemically dangerous, dirty, physically demanding, and intellectually deadening. A more vigorous material equality and a correspondingly more authentic range of consent will not be the end of what Michael Walzer refers to by the plain term "hard work."[2]

To be sure, much of today's work is soft in contrast with the past. Thanks to industrial productivity, technological cleverness, and the movement of jobs abroad, we have eradicated a great deal of the back-breaking and mind-numbing labor that gave work a bad name.[3] The simple matter of washing clothes (a two-day project just for one couple's laundry in the nineteenth century) is now a minor inconvenience, requiring little raw physical toil. And as we abuse our bodies less in the business of getting by and getting ahead, so we are likely to develop our minds more. Today's economy is increasingly characterized by managerial and professional work—"symbolic analysts," to use Robert Reich's category.[4] This work emphasizes the manipulation of symbols, whether they are the zeros and ones of computer programmers, the careful clauses of lawyers, the subtle images of graphic artists, or the models of research scientists. More generally it includes the conceptual identification of problems and their solutions and the arts of negotiation and brokering. Yet along with such work (which occupies no more than 20 percent of the American labor force) there remains much more work of a familiar sort: service sector jobs and manufacturing jobs. Together these make up more than 50 percent of American jobs.[5]

The promise of our economy is that we will educate citizens such that many more might participate in the economy of symbolic analysts. In that case we ought to ask how large this category might become. Might it double, triple—could everyone be a symbolic analyst? Perhaps this could happen, with some technological marvel we have not yet imagined, something more far reaching in its transformative potential than the computer revolution or the information superhighway. Short of a technological fix that renders many familiar forms of human labor obsolete, the increase in symbolic analytic work at home would seem to depend on exporting the work we shun, or on importing workers to carry out those remaining unpleasant tasks that future Americans will be too educated and too proud to perform themselves. So the hierarchy of work, where some do more attractive work than others, persists. Perhaps it is from a recognition of this that nonutopian liberals like Gutmann and Thompson insist that work cannot be stripped of its obligatory character.

The inequalities we most readily recognize involve income, status, authority, and power. Since these usually correlate positively with one another, together they constitute a core aspect of the inequality besetting liberal capitalist societies. Yet the quality of work itself involves a hierarchy less talked about, and less noticed. Work is not equal in what it offers intrinsically, and apart from inequalities of income, status, and authority, there remains an inequality in the distribution of meaningful, rewarding, intrinsically gratifying work. Some perform jobs that develop their talents and actualize their energies, while others do jobs of a more mundane or painful sort. Ideal consent given under perfect conditions of freedom and equality will not eradicate the hierarchy of work. Meanwhile actual or everyday consent can shield the hierarchy of work from critical scrutiny: the jobs people have (and the advantages or penalties those jobs carry) are justified, one might say, so long as individuals freely consent to them. In contrast to this, ideals like meaningful work, or more generally fitting work, expose the hierarchy of work to deeper examination.

Demeaning Work

To make this more concrete it may help to descend from the ideal of consent (which we would give in a perfectly fair situation to the basic structure of society) and consider the actual consent that people give to particular jobs. For it is in the context of actual consent that the standard of fitting work becomes most urgent. Take, for instance, the work of bathroom attendants, a job now only occasionally seen in the United States. Studs Terkel interviewed a man who attended the washroom in one of the great Chicago hotels, offering hand towels, Vitalis, Aqua Velva, even eye drops. Although all come, sooner or later, to appreciate a clean bathroom, this attendant suggested that the essential purpose of his job was to make the hotel guests, when they visited the washroom, feel important. The attendant knew this job had no purpose other than to give hotel patrons a chance to feel tall and superior. Noting that he was not proud of his work, the man said, "The whole thing is obsolete. It's on its way out. This work isn't necessary in the first place."[6] Yet the obsolescence is subtle; the work, after all, was not recently displaced by some technological innovation. Rather, the role's obsolescence stems from its conflict with democratic pride, which *ought* to have rendered the work obsolete by rendering shameful the desire of some to look down on others. What was obsolete was the underlying notion that some exist to serve the petty desires of others.

Work roles that exist solely to give some the opportunity to look *down* cannot be said to fit the purposes of democratic citizens. From the perspective of actual or nominal consent, there is nothing at all wrong with such work; indeed the presence of such options is to be commended, for without them we can assume that the man Terkel interviewed would be worse off. Even from the perspective of fair consent to the basic structure of society, we cannot say that anything is wrong with the job role itself. Perhaps such work is voluntary and even adds to economic efficiency. Perhaps too, in a society regulated by the difference principle, there would be no takers for such a job; or perhaps there would be. Only by assessing the role in terms of its fit—in this case with the sense of dignity and equality that democracies cultivate—can we make sense of the attendant's complaint as a matter of moral importance.

To make sense of the complaint in terms of fit is not to conclude that the role should be abolished. To warrant that conclusion, the fit would need to be so bad that the job would constitute an assault on "the human form of life."[7] Rather than conclude that whatever does not fit individuals well should be therefore abolished, the standard of fit serves to interrupt the complacency that a premature satisfaction with the fact of consent would support. If consent is the only regulative ideal on the justice of work, then there is less reason to take as problematic job roles that exist only to satisfy pretensions of superiority. If such roles are understood to be problematic—as considerations of fit would indicate—then a range of options might be entertained short of simply abolishing them. These include, for instance, redefining them such that they are oriented more toward the provision of useful services and less toward the satisfaction of inegalitarian pretensions. These options, however, become pressing only if the standard of fit is taken as relevant alongside the more familiar standard of consent.

Another example concerns contemporary objections to sweatshop labor, where this is understood to refer to working conditions with no floor on wages and no limit on working hours. Sweatshops also may include unsafe conditions, physical and sexual violence, restraints on the right of exit, and even brute coercion. Although such conditions have been uncovered in workplaces in a number of American cities, they are more often found in export industries located in countries whose comparative advantage is the presence of an impoverished multitude willing to work for pennies an hour. Among others, many students in recent years have objected to trade with foreign sweatshops. They aim not to abolish such trade but to press consumers and manufacturers to enforce basic standards of safety and hygiene, as well as wage floors, on foreign suppliers.

Insofar as trade across borders is concerned, arguments based on fair consent to the basic structure of one's society might not apply. Rawls's principles of justice, which pay particular attention to the fortunes of the least advantaged, apply more obviously within one society than around the globe.[8] At the same time, the standard of actual consent would, it seems, offer a qualified celebration of sweatshop labor. It would not justify the arrangements akin to slavery, or violence, or restrictions on the right of exit, for all of these would undermine the voluntariness that is the key assurance of mutual benefit. But beyond this restriction, the standard of actual consent would defend all voluntary contracts because they involve mutual benefit. Workers in Guatemala are made better off stitching clothes at the *maquila,* as children in Pakistan making soccer balls are made richer than they could otherwise be, this argument goes. Workers are often "banging at the gates of the 'sweatshops' for a chance of entry."[9] At the same time, consumers in affluent countries are made better off by the availability of cheaper goods. Given that no one is coerced and that the arrangements produce mutual benefit, sweatshop work is in a sense commendable, in this argument.

Any argument for simply abolishing trade with foreign sweatshops must take stock of the brutal fact that such a restriction would leave the world's worst off even poorer. At the same time, aside from coercion the standard of consent alone cannot account for why "this issue is of extraordinary moral magnitude."[10] A concern with fit (in this case, with a basic fit that addresses the conditions of human functioning) helps account for the moral concern that consent as an everyday regulative ideal cannot identify. The problem with monotonous work that is also unbounded—that has no limits on hours—is that it leaves no space for the development of basic human capacities. This alone does not justify abolishing trade or imposing such costs that foreign labor cannot compete internationally; fit itself is not a complete standard that crowds out every other. Considerations of fit should not therefore be invoked in clumsy ways that salve the moral pretensions of the advantaged while punishing the world's least advantaged.[11] However, the category of fit does make sense of the morally problematic nature of sweatshop work, even when it is carried on abroad and even when it is voluntary and mutually beneficial. Fit offers a moral vocabulary that allows us to articulate why we see sweatshop labor as an assault on human dignity. As such, it can animate and justify efforts to enforce basic standards of safety, hygiene, rest, and wage floors in ways that preserve the mutual benefits that accrue through international trade.

Consent cannot fully capture the concerns we bring to the evaluation of the economy and work. When companies that have long resided in particular communities suddenly close their operations and move jobs elsewhere in search of lower labor costs, the change is met not only with expressions of futility—as if the forces exacting greater efficiency cannot long be resisted—but also with a sense of betrayal. When layoffs, restructurings, and plant closings occur, the lament has much to do with money and security; but these are never the whole story, nor does the common interest in both fully account for the betrayal and sadness that accompany the ravages of downsizing.[12] Sadness over the passing of manufacturing jobs and the movement of jobs to low-wage areas reveals not only an interest in money and security but also the belief that the relationship to work ought to be characterized by something stronger than consent, which might be renounced in a moment's time. The moral aspects of these relationships, which often involve loyalty, identification, and commitment, are distorted when described only in the language of consent.

At an individual level, people seek work that is not merely acceptable but also appropriate and good. Many turn to the language of fit when evaluating their work: "That job," one might say, "was a bad fit; I decided to look for something else." This language reflects the need for some standard that can guide individual choices by describing some commitments as more appropriate and worthwhile than others. Thinking about work in these terms marks a notable change from two generations ago. In today's world of work, where for better and for worse we no longer find the bargain of old—loyalty in exchange for job security—where we must make choices and shoulder risks standing alone, where nearly all participate in the world of work, it is hard to avoid thinking about work in terms of fit.[13]

Two generations past, for instance, the bargain with work focused more exclusively on the basics: security, pay, and benefits. To get a good deal—steady work, incremental raises, and a job packed with benefits—required not that one fit one's job but that one "fit in," where this meant conforming to the ethos of the organization. To fit in meant suppressing one's individuality in favor of compliance, conformity, and devotion. Social critics of the time viewed the conformity of the corporate world with alarm, worried that independence was sacrificed to the soulless obedience of the "organization man."[14] Instead of conformity, today's world of work demands flexibility in the face of insecurity and change. Faced with the real prospect of changing firms or careers, workers need to consider how the competencies they develop through work form a portfolio that might be marketed elsewhere. Today's workers are called on to relate more immediately to the actual work they do, and to consider how this fits with their aptitudes and their purposes. The task today is not so much to fit in as to find work that fits us.

The aspiration to find work that fits is no longer the mark only of dreamy romantics but rather emanates from contemporary conditions of the working life. These conditions, of course, do not apply to everyone: they are concentrated among those who have choices, who are at some remove from the desperation that makes any job attractive. The following description of today's working life is noteworthy not because it is universally valid but because it points to ideals of work that have wide influence and implications for the meaning and justice of work. Ideals like fitting work have gained particular urgency because of the way that the contemporary economy situates individuals in a direct and immediate relation to market forces.

The Immediate Relationship to the Market

Working life today is less likely than in the past to be mediated by binding affiliations with institutions like unions and large institutions. Individuals have a more immediate relationship to their job, to the market, and to the risks that markets impose. The decline in unions since 1950, for instance, has been profound. Although most people approve of unions, now only 14 percent of those in the labor force belong to one.[15] At the same time, as corporations extend less job security, they also elicit less in the way of identification and loyalty. The trends toward outsourcing and downsizing in the 1980s and 1990s killed off much of what remained of the midcentury's "organization man." Although workers may not generally work in fear that their job will end tomorrow, most know that any job might be sacrificed to the next market transition or tough patch in corporate profits.[16] A senseless turn of the market index, a shift in corporate strategy, a surprise merger, a new source of cheaper labor—that is all it takes to put one back in the job search.[17] Education, connections, and developed skills may cushion the blow, but they are no insurance against it.[18] The new world of work contains few affiliations that protect against downside risk, few islands of safety to be settled.

This more immediate work relationship has a consequence for wages. In the old world of work, wages often correlated more with the organization than with the job role. A secretary at IBM made an IBM salary. Job security, too, came with a good alliance. To be connected to a large and stable corporation or a powerful union brought a measure of security. Such institutional alliances ironed out risks: they made employment steady and wages predictable.[19] Today the risks of work fall more squarely on the individual, and pay reflects job roles rather than institutional alliances. A secretary makes a secretary's salary, whether at IBM or elsewhere, and the gaps between different roles in the same organization are wider today than at any time in the past several decades.[20] As a result, no longer do young people of ambition aim primarily to hitch their fate to a single large and protective organization. Rather, changing jobs is common—and sometimes lucrative.[21] This is most obvious among the most advantaged. Where professionals were once defined by loyalty to the firm, today lawyers, for instance, commonly leave their firm for a larger share of the bounty next door—or are fired when they fail to generate enough business.[22] As with lawyers, so with professionals generally; it is no surprise to see engineers, programmers, marketers, agents, or administrative assistants change employers, either from necessity or for the promise of something better elsewhere.

Yet the erosion of institutional affiliations that offered some protection against market risk has left all but the most advantaged more vulnerable. As individuals bear the risks of work more immediately, so the distance between those who win and those who lose has increased in comparison with the economy of fifty years ago. To some, these changes signal a more meritocratic organization of work, since jobs and pay reflect market forces more than they reflect one's standing in a bureaucratic organization. Working for a "good company" matters less (as do a good name, the right look, and family connections), while the value individuals bring to work on their own matters more. This is not to say that merit, however it is understood, is everything. It is not by merit alone that one finds oneself in a losing division or a hot sector. The deeper change in the world of work is not simply that it is more meritocratic, but that what counts as merit has changed.

In steady times, when risks are predictable and manageable, the relevant merit is a conformity with preexisting expectation and custom, an ability to "fill the shoes" of those who came before.[23] When risks are less predictable, not conformity but "flexibility" is lauded. This flexibility includes the ability to adapt to expansive job definitions, as well as the ability to acquire skills that are in demand as markets change. More abstractly, flexibility is the ability to massage fate, to respond adeptly and resourcefully to variety and change in ways that conduce to one's advantage. Work that asks us to be flexible does not hem us in or structure our behavior with unrelenting discipline; it rather offers—or insists on—some latitude in the range of responses we exhibit. Variety and change impose their own burdens, but these are distinct from those that come with the rigid roles and fixed structures long associated with industrial or bureaucratic work. We might celebrate the freedom that comes with flexibility, for it preserves some space between worker and work, and accommodates the autonomy that individuals exhibit as they respond to change and variety.

Playful Work

Amid the celebration of the "new economy," some conceive of ideal work as a form of play. Unlike the conforming, loyal "man in the gray flannel suit," who by glad-handing and good cheer worked his way into a stable bureaucratic order, the successful players in the new economy are audacious, committed, and fun loving. Michael Lewis, in his portrait of the entrepreneur Jim Clark (founder of Silicon Graphics and Netscape), defines the new economy's heroes.[24] Creative and impulsive, they take risks. Self-defining, they bristle at the suggestion that work defines them. They embrace change—and lack patience. This is elaborated in Po Bronson's description of Silicon Valley in the 1990s high-tech boom.[25] Bronson chronicled characters who work hard more from passion than habit or fear, who aim to break out on their own rather than establish a safe place in the big organization. They are proud of this passion and subtly scorn those in whom it is lacking. Lewis and Bronson looked only to the winners of the technological economy, at a time when winnings were large, but their descriptions carry a point: winners of the new economy have found work that is like play.

Yet the playfulness some prize seems as much born of disappointment as of hope. Insofar as playful work is experienced as cynical and transient, it represents more of an escape than an embrace. By creating an ironic distance between work and worker, this sort of playfulness protects one from the *Dilbert*-like senselessness of the workplace more than it engages one in the flow of an absorbing activity. For instance, the editors of *Gig* (a compilation of interviews done in the 1990s with people about their work) argue that in contrast to the work ethic depicted in Studs Terkel's 1972 book *Working*, the ethic now is "more casual, transitory, cynical, and playful."[26] This ironic temperament resists the suggestion that the world might be remade in the image of any grand ideology—yet also disdains enchantment with the world as it is. *This* sort of playfulness is safe; it takes the advantages it inherits for granted, and forgoes risk. Edgy without being critical, this temperament is not often earnest: declarations are always modified, serious moments leavened by a knowing wink. Moreover, real commitments like work are made to seem less real by viewing them as a sort of game, or play.

To see work as play in this sense is to defend oneself from disappointment by isolating work in a self-contained (safely distant) place. Of course, the reality of work is that it is often set apart from the rest of life. Work is truncated from the family, not only taking place in a distinct location but also following norms that would be out of place at home. Play is an apt metaphor when work seems like a game that, however unpleasant, is disconnected from the larger society. In these respects, the fragmentation of work makes work more like play: its meaning is self-contained. To think of our work as play in this sense is to find some protection from the insults, the stupidity, and the insecurity of the workplace.

Yet idealizing work as play gets much wrong. Ironic distance makes us observe as if we do not also participate. While it allows us to see ourselves and our work from a distance, it also threatens to insert too much distance between worker and work by supposing that we could be wholly unserious about work. This overlooks the real pain and trial, and the real satisfaction and hope that make up the experience of work. For most, work is not something occasional or a matter of dabbling. Cynical or ironic playfulness is an escape from reality—a temporary solace perhaps, but not an ideal of the working life. Even the editors of *Gig,* who find today's work ethic less earnest and more playful than in the past, seem to ignore the examples their book offers. A UPS driver, for instance, reports, "But usually, when I'm out there, I just do everything I can to not actually work." *Gig* does offer examples of some who love their work, but even here the image of playfulness cannot account for the seriousness of their devotion, as in the case of the trial lawyer who sacrificed a marriage, his health, and sleep to a job he loves. Nor does play express the sense of limitation, of unfreedom, that comes with work—in its most extreme, this is expressed by the assembly-line worker who finds his job "like a prison sentence."[27] The editors of *Gig* overlook the frustration and fragmentation of work that come from low pay, job insecurity, and shortsighted management for the freedom that comes from experiencing work as play.

If the market's demand to be flexible carries a threat to our integrity, the distance of ironic play fails to offer sufficient protection. No one is infinitely flexible; to be wholly accommodating is to dissolve one's center and erase all the boundaries that mark who one is. Faced with the erosion of rigid job definitions and life-long institutional loyalties, individuals are compelled not only to be flexible, but also to articulate the boundaries of their flexibility. They need to think carefully about how they relate to the actual activity of their work. As specific job descriptions and organizational structures offer fewer constraints and less guidance, individuals are driven to think for themselves about how they fit their work. In contrast to the distance that ironic play interposes between self and work, this response to the demand for flexibility attempts to draw the connection between worker and work more closely.[28]

This points to a second understanding of playful work, as being less an escape from reality than a kind of absorption *in* reality. Here playfulness does not distance worker from work but deeply engages the two. Playful work in this more demanding sense involves achieving a kind of "flow," in which we are adequately challenged, experience intense concentration, and are so engrossed that we lose awareness of time passing and even of "a self separate from the world around it."[29] Jobs can provide an opportunity for play in this sense when they are akin to games, "with variety, appropriate and flexible challenges, clear goals, and immediate feedback."[30] In this sort of playful work we do not move willy-nilly from one thing to another, but instead we practice and develop competencies. This work involves discipline and commitment, yet is not always experienced as a constraint. It *feels,* in a way, fun. Work and play in this sense have much in common: nominally antonyms, the elementary opposition relaxes when play is at its most serious and work is at its most absorbing.[31]

This sort of play requires something of both work and worker. Not every kind of work will offer the same opportunities for absorbing play: surgery offers more opportunity for the "flow experience" than the assembly line. Yet not every surgeon will be able to experience the work as absorbing play; this also requires a certain kind of individual, one who is capable of recognizing opportunities for action. One needs to be playful, in a sense, with one's surroundings, transforming the mundane into something more game-like, revealing (for oneself) opportunities for action where others see only routine. With an orientation that equips one to take advantage of the opportunities, "even the most mundane job can enhance the quality of life, rather than detract from it."[32] In this ideal of playful work, irony does not impose a distance between work and worker, making the strains of work comically bearable; instead, a playful spirit engages work by seeking opportunities for challenge and satisfaction.

However, even the most playful spirits encounter limits: playful work is rarely as fun as playful play. Even those who succeed in finding satisfying challenges at work, who say they are often "in the flow" while working, also report that they would rather be doing something else.[33] The ideal of playful work captures something that work at its best has in common with play, but it overlooks the discipline and limitation (one might say compulsion) that adhere to the experience of work. If the model of playful work captures many of the features we wish for in our work, it can exaggerate the extent to which work, even at its best, is wholly voluntary or perfectly free. Playful work that is engaging, that enlists our concentration and offers its own satisfactions, points less to perfect freedom than to fit. The ideal of fitting work, like the playful work, involves an engagement between work and worker. Yet fitting work acknowledges the way work limits our freedom. To fit something is to have the possibility of *not* fitting something else: the idea of fit admits that we have boundaries, that there are some things, however desirable, we do not fit, whether by nature, habit, or inclination. At the same time, fitting work carries the promise, like playful work, of fulfillment.

The demands of flexibility and the promise of fulfillment together invite people to focus on the match or the fit between worker and work. Because fit is elusive, and because so much depends on the way a particular individual relates to a particular kind of activity, career advice centers on helping people find their fit. To locate our right fit requires, according to one strain of this advice, that we take stock of not only what makes money but also our passions. "The very first step to finding work that fits you," says one book of career advice, "is to understand what you love."[34] The emphasis is on self-understanding: "Concentrate on who you are, and the rest will fall into place."[35] This means unlocking an authentic self by hewing to activities we find "most engaging and natural."[36] In finding our fit, the stakes are high: "It is true that if one finds flow in work, and in relations to other people, one is well on the way toward improving the quality of life as a whole."[37] "Every aspect of your life," another advisor says, "is directly related to how well your career fits you."[38]

Affirming the Working Life

The notion of fitting work as an integral part of a life well lived reflects a deeper affirmation of the working life. If work is in part a painful necessity, it is also thought to be (especially in the United

States) part of a good life, connected to responsibility, social recognition, identity, and fulfillment. In the belief that work is good, America today stands apart from the earlier progressive goal of abolishing work. According to the utopian hopes of an earlier age, productivity, social cooperation, and political reform would render the rigor, discipline, and pain of work a thing of the past. In its place, people could enjoy a more natural, spontaneous, less willful approach to life. Marx, for instance, thought that the collective control of capital would not only end exploitation—where some by their power co-opt the value others create—but would also liberate people from the confinement of work roles. In the remarkable image depicted by Marx, we could hunt in the morning, fish in the afternoon, rear cattle in the evening, and criticize after dinner, without being dominated or defined by one role, without becoming a hunter, fisherman, rancher, or critic.[39] Bertrand Russell, a more "ambivalent socialist," also hoped that industrial productivity would make leisure universal, no longer the reward of aristocratic luck.[40] Indeed, for much of the past century, the habit of hard work has lacked the respect of intellectuals, especially those on the left. Following Weber, many saw it as an unhappy trap set by early fanatical Protestants and held tight by the unrelenting pressure of economic competition under capitalism.[41] Today some still celebrate the promise of a workless future.[42]

The hope of escaping work may be in part a futuristic fantasy, but it has also been based in a sound appreciation of the pain entailed in the worst forms of work, as also in a more fundamental assessment of the bad fit between work in general and the promise of humanity. Against the expressive potential of humanity, work imposes an ugly discipline. Yet today in the United States, this view is on the margins; the thrust of contemporary politics is not to generalize leisure but to enable and even require participation in the paid economy. Once, critics of the old welfare system acknowledged that some jobs make work a bad deal—they give more to the society than they give to the individuals who perform them. Today the same critics are more likely to affirm the value of work for those who do it, regardless of what they do.

For instance, Lawrence Mead, in an influential case for work incentives, notes that, "A higher proportion of Americans than ever before appear to derive much of their satisfaction in life from their jobs. Employment has become a dominant source of personal identity and meaning as well as income."[43] While Mead attributes poverty to individual habits and conduct, even those who stress the social and structural factors that motivate joblessness agree about the value of work. The "disappearance of work and the consequences of that disappearance for both social and cultural life are the central problems in the inner-city ghetto," argues William Julius Wilson.[44] And President Clinton, in supporting the 1996 welfare reform act, stated that work "gives structure, meaning and dignity to most of our lives."[45] Indeed, for many the single most important goal of welfare reform was "getting people into the workforce."[46]

Part of the contemporary case for work rests on its obligatory character. As we saw in the last chapter, work is one of the most powerful ways in which ordinary citizens contribute to the larger society.[47] But the case for work is also grounded in the belief that work imposes a salutary discipline: work imposes a regularity on life that cuts against the sway of passing and unruly desire. If the daily discipline of work may dampen the spirit, it also keeps poverty at bay. For those who must live only by their hands and wits, the habit of work is prudent. Yet the contemporary affirmation of work goes beyond social obligation, discipline, and prudence. Work gives us not only structure but also, as Clinton says, "meaning and dignity." It is a source not only of income but also of "personal identity."

One small indication that our affirmation of work rests on more than prudence is found in the fact that Americans work even when they do not have to. The wealthy, for instance, see their advantage more in finding good work than in escaping the world of work. More than 90 percent of those with a net worth of more than 2.5

million dollars continue to work and earn; riches, it appears, do not put an end to work.[48] More revealing, most insist that were they to become wealthy, they would continue to work.[49] Only the retired enjoy permanent respite from work, and even if this comes (for some) earlier in the life cycle than it did in the past, its social legitimacy nonetheless depends on its following many years spent at work.[50]

The working life is the life Americans live and affirm. Work is what structures most people's time; the working life is the dominant way of life, and no one characterizes this condition as degrading or debilitating. On the contrary, work (rather than the wealth that equips one to avoid working) is essential to the social standing of citizens.[51] As a general feature of American society, this affirmation of the working life is nothing new. As we will later see, the early Protestants upended the old belief that saintliness required insulation from the activities of ordinary life, instead insisting that religious devotion is expressed in diligence at a calling.[52] This was intensified in the democratic culture of the Jacksonians, who thought only the working life honest, and all honest work honorable.[53] Amid the growing affluence of the late twentieth century, the affirmation of the working life has only solidified.

The affirmation of the working life may be motivated by a sense that work in general is fitting—it gives support to our dignity and secures our happiness. In this respect, we affirm work from a spirit of generosity, hoping that no one is "exiled" from the accomplishment and reward only working brings. Or the affirmation of work could reflect more resentment than generosity. Because we know that, as often as not, work stunts, misdirects, and constrains us in ways that are deleterious to our development, we seek to impose work on those who might otherwise escape it. In this way, the contemporary affirmation of the working life leads us to consider how work fits and what fitting work is.

Intuitively, fitting work is clear enough: to say, "that job is a good fit" signals both that one does it well and that to some degree one thrives in doing it well. Yet doing a job well and thriving in it are very different, and this difference points to two distinct understandings of fit. The first involves possessing the aptitudes that enable us to carry out jobs that society needs performed. In this case, what we fit are the tasks that society generates: by virtue of fitting our work, we are useful to others and contribute to the society. All useful work involves some fit between our dispositions, skills, and talents, on one hand, and the needs and wants of others, on the other. This fit is important, so far as it goes: that work contributes to the common good is a central part of its justice.

But it is always possible that we might do useful work, and even do it well, yet experience it as dull, meaningless, repetitive, or deadening. This possibility points to the second understanding of fit, which is central to Chapters 5 through 8. This concept of fit is more emphatically centered on the individual and involves a harmonious alignment between the processes and purposes we engage in at work and something distinctively our own, such as our own goals, values, or good development. The tension between serving social needs and serving our own purposes is at the heart of the problem of meaningful work. Must contributing to society come at the cost of the freedom to tend to our own purposes?

The next chapter examines the ancient understandings of fitting work found in the thought of Plato and Aristotle. We turn to the ancients not only because they wrote explicitly about fitting work but also because they help answer whether a concern with fit bears a threat to freedom. Plato and Aristotle conceived of the justice of work more in terms of fit than freedom. Aristotle argued that some human beings were fitted to even the worst sort of work—that of the slave—and that it would be just to force such people to fill the role of the slave. More generally, he thought of fitting work with reference to a hierarchical ranking of human capacities: each is fit to the sort of work that best develops his or her highest capacities. This ordering of human capacities would seem to undermine freedom by imputing social purposes to persons regardless of what they would choose or endorse. As the following chapter shows, the concept of fit need not mean that there is one proper end for each person, nor does it necessitate a narrow conception of human capacities that would undermine a commitment to choice and freedom. Rather it asserts that *each* person, by the particular nature he or she bears, has a claim that justice cannot overlook.

3

The Justice of Fit

An ideal of fitting work has roots in both contemporary conditions of economic life and the culture of American democracy. Yet as a category of political and moral analysis, the concept of fit should arouse deep suspicion, for it seems more at home in an aristocratic society of fixed places than in a liberal society of equal opportunity and "shifting involvements," where freedom and consent would seem more appropriate ideals.[1] In an aristocratic society of fixed "stations," individuals do not so much choose their roles as they are recruited, assigned, and coerced. Those on top bear most of the responsibility for great decisions; they chart the course and give direction to the rest. A few steps down are managerial types, who accept direction from above and direct those below. Still further down are those with no one to manage, who have only to execute and obey. In the aristocratic view, each link in the social chain is necessary and important, though each is not equally authoritative, honorable, or desirable. To those who conceive of society in such a way, the task of politics is to somehow manipulate or force individuals to occupy their appropriate social roles—and keep them there.

A conception of fit is integral to such a hierarchical view of social order: society is properly ordered when all do the work to which they are fitted, even if this requires manipulation and coercion. One of the most notorious examples of this view comes from Aristotle, who argues in *The Politics* that certain human beings are fitted to slavery, and that slavery is just when these individuals occupy the role. In this light, the concept of fit seems to stand squarely against the modern affirmation of human freedom and equality. Nonetheless, a concern with fitting work does not undercut the interest in equal respect and freedom at the core of modern liberal democracy. On the contrary, the concept of fit can corroborate and support these values. To demonstrate this more fully, this chapter turns to the place where the ideal of fit may seem most opposed to liberal and democratic prepossessions, the hierarchical and aristocratic views found in the political thought of Plato and Aristotle.

That we do not share many of the ancients' assumptions (principally their profound moral inegalitarianism) amplifies rather than undermines their utility. Because we do not share all their commitments, confronting them can reveal something of the partiality and incompleteness of our own assumptions—as it can also deepen and make more explicit the conviction with which we hold our own commitments. In particular, looking to Plato and Aristotle shows how a concern with fit can be consistent with the moral reasons that give freedom and consent such force. This becomes particularly evident when we consider the distinct emphases Plato and Aristotle each place in their considerations of fitting work. We find in Plato an emphasis on social fit, which involves work's contribution to the common good. In its most unqualified form, social fit might even justify coercing individuals to perform socially necessary sorts of work. This is the view that Aristotle considers in his analysis of slavery—the injustice of which, in his view, depends on looking beyond social needs to what individuals, taken by themselves, deserve. By invoking what individuals deserve, Aristotle pointedly issues a demanding understanding of fit, one that places even contemporary work under a heavy justificatory burden. The category of fit more effectively challenged than defended the hierarchy Aristotle examined. But before turning to Aristotle, I will first briefly consider Plato's *Republic,* where the category of fit seems to justify manipulation and constraint and is invoked for the sake of keeping people in their place. Plato, as we will see, gives more emphasis to what cities need than to what individuals by their nature deserve.

Plato's Simple City

The most familiar understanding of fit involves an alignment of individual aptitudes and tasks. Indeed, this is the sort of fit that defines the simple city of Plato's *Republic.* The simple city is dedicated to satisfying all the most basic needs, and only those needs. Nothing done is unneeded, and nothing unneeded is done. Yet even this simple city exhibits a division of labor, since when people specialize they do a "finer job," Socrates says, than they would as generalists. For this city to be just, the division of labor must not be arbitrary, which is to say that it must reflect real individual differences rather than create social differences. There needs to be a reason that explains why it is right for this or that particular person to be a shoemaker, for instance. This reason, according to Socrates in *The Republic,* is rooted in differences in natural aptitude. Each of us, he says, "is naturally not quite like anyone else, but rather differs in his nature; different men are apt for the accomplishment of different jobs."[2]

But even in the simple city, some jobs are more desirable than others. Socrates' interlocutor Adeimantus, for instance, worries that selling in the marketplace—a job he takes to be tedious and repetitive—is both wasteful and boring. This worry raises the question: who gets the good, desirable work, and who the tedious, or hard work? In the simple city, the matter of distributing good and bad work depends on social fit. In "rightly governed cities," Socrates says, those whose bodies are useless for other tasks would be tradesmen; similarly, those of weak mind and strong body would be laborers. Social fit does *not* require that each does the thing he or she does best in the absolute sense. Steve may be better at building than at growing, yet be quite superb at both. And Sally may be an incompetent grower and an average builder. The right social fit here is that Steve be the grower and Sally the builder. Although Steve does not do what he does best in the absolute sense, this arrangement maximizes their contribution to the social needs.

The contribution to social needs is what makes social fit not merely a guide to individual choice but also a matter of justice. Where work is fitting in this social sense, each person contributes optimally to the common good. Should one ask, "Why am *I* a shoemaker?" the answer would be, "Because that is how you can best serve the common good." Service to the city gives the distribution of roles its justification and also explains why certain individuals fill certain roles. Perfect social fit points to an ideal of an organic society, where for every social need, no matter how boring or hard, there is someone who by natural aptitude best fits the task. Yet in practice, social fit always falls short of the utopian ideal depicted in Plato's simple city.

Even in the imaginary city of *The Republic,* achieving the rudimentary fit between individuals and the tasks social life makes necessary is not easy. It demands both an intrusive education and a perspicacious discernment of individual aptitudes. In the end, a public lie is needed to justify the distribution of roles. Part of Plato's famous "noble lie" claims that the individuals composing the several classes of the city are distinguished at birth by metals mixed in their souls, and these metals signify the jobs to which each is suited.[3] Yet the invocation of such a myth raises an important question: if the individuals in fact deserve their roles by virtue of their natural aptitude, why the lie?

The lie might be an act of rhetoric or persuasion that starts from a false premise (metals mixed with souls) in order to convince people of a true conclusion (that some deserve better roles and others worse roles). The lie is necessary to persuade individuals to *accept* only that to which they are suited by aptitude. Yet denying the limits of our aptitude is common: we can easily enough convince ourselves of an exaggerated assessment of our own talent. We also often resist what we are best at, and pursue with ardor what we wish we could do while forsaking what we can in fact accomplish. We fail to recognize our limits both because we are proud and because when we are relatively bad at something we are also often bad judges of its quality. The noble lie recognizes this tendency to mistake what we are good at, to reject the limits of our talent, and to insist on doing what we cannot do well.

Aside from the difficulty of judging ourselves accurately and restricting ourselves to the limits of our aptitude, the noble lie points to a deeper problem with social fit. The lie confesses that, often, doing what we are aptitudinally suited for (from the perspective of social need) does not make us happy. We may reject living within the limits of our aptitude because what we are good at, relative to others, is also something unfulfilling with respect to ourselves. An excellent accountant may fail to find much pleasure or meaning in the task. In *The Republic* it is again a comment by Adeimantus that suggests this problem. In the very simple city, where only rudimentary needs are filled, there is little enjoyment. When everyone lives only for the city and not for themselves, the discipline of a division of labor looks pointless. Artisans and farmers toil from youth on so that the warriors might be educated, but no one seems to have a desirable life. Even those on top of the city's hierarchy—especially those—do not live happily, to Adeimantus's eye.[4]

Adeimantus's objection reminds us that performing the tasks that society requires, even when we perform them efficiently and wonderfully, is no guarantee that we as individuals will thrive. Unless we take the city's prosperity and health as identical with our own, there is no reason to take our bearings only from the common good. To count ourselves as worthy independent of the common good is normal and right. Even the nobility of sacrifice in the name of the common good presupposes the distinction between what is good for society and what is good for us as individuals. Social fit, especially in its extreme forms, asks for too much sacrifice. As

Adeimantus saw, social fit overprivileges the city as it neglects the individual. This is why it offers an incomplete account of the justice of work: it takes stock of the need to contribute to the common good, but does not pay sufficient attention to what individuals deserve.

Markets and Social Fit

This is not to say that the goal of aligning individual aptitudes with the tasks society needs is mistaken. On the contrary, it is essential. Not only Plato's imaginary city but every city—every group that cooperates for the sake of common ends like security and comfort—needs to achieve some level of social fit. In Plato's city, social fit is achieved through politics: it requires a lie issued at the city's founding, and relies on political power to assign individuals to their roles. In contemporary politics, we take it that no such lie is necessary, that no visible political power is needed to compel individuals to fill their roles. Instead, individuals choose against a background of the market, which we trust will secure an optimal social fit between persons and roles. As with the social fit of Plato's *Republic,* one justification of markets is not that they give individuals all they deserve, but instead that they recruit individuals to roles in a way that optimizes production toward social needs.

Those who defend free markets argue that wages, for instance, should correspond to neither individual effort nor need nor the moral quality of individual character considered more broadly. Friedrich Hayek, for instance, claims that wages should instead reflect contribution understood as "the advantage we derive from what others offer us." In this view, by rewarding the perceived value that one's efforts have for others, free markets result in a "maximum of usefulness."[5] Markets do this by achieving an optimal social fit between persons and jobs. Without markets, "How is it to be decided who is to be the doctor, who the lawyer, who the garbage collector, who the street sweeper," ask Milton and Rose Friedman. Short of free markets, they argue, "only force or the threat of force will do."[6] Functionalist sociologists of midcentury argued the same, holding that wage differentials attract people of the requisite talents to jobs that are functionally important to society. Doctors make more than street sweepers, on this view, because society needs to entice those of the right talent to undergo years of arduous education and training.[7] The market performs the same function as the wise rulers in Plato's *Republic*, but without the lies, the indoctrination, and the elaborate contrivances Plato described.

The success of markets at solving the problem of social fit without recourse to brute coercion is a crucial part of their legitimacy. Our faith, a faith read back to Adam Smith and confirmed in the collapse of the communist economies, is that market forces will define jobs and recruit individuals to those jobs in such a way that neither any redistribution nor redefinition of jobs could make the economy more productive. While this faith has been amply supported by experience, the social fit markets achieve is never perfect. On the contrary, in a variety of ways they fail to optimally match individual skill and talent to tasks. For instance, windfall wages in some sectors can attract a disproportionate share of talent: too many, from a social point of view, may aim to be "master of the universe" investment bankers or Academy Award–winning stars. At the same time, markets may fail to offer enough opportunity to the less skilled—especially when firms can easily move operations abroad.[8] What markets elicit is never identical to the common good, because markets function to satisfy the demand (whatever it is) of those who can afford satisfaction. The satisfaction of wants may or may not be good for society: the trade in weapons, for instance, and the market for gambling on scratch cards contribute nothing to society and yet are profitable. Sometimes socially important work receives little or no market reward because those who directly benefit cannot afford to pay for it. Banking services in poor neighborhoods and childcare services are ready examples.

But the more central problem with the justice of markets is similar to the problem of Plato's social fit. As the social fit of Plato's simple city gave insufficient consideration to what individuals deserve, so market wages are vulnerable to the same objection. They direct effort to social needs, but they do not offer a very profound reason for an individual to do this sort of work rather than that. They say nothing about why a person should find work meaningful or fulfilling, or about why it is an appropriate expression of one's identity. All that markets can offer is a wage. Wages give people an incentive to do this job rather than that, and they offer a convincing sign that our work makes a contribution (someone, after all, is willing to pay). But they neither establish much of a connection between one's identity and one's work nor, by necessity, do they adequately reflect the social contribution of work.

From the dawn of the industrial age many have recognized that market wages fail to adequately recognize the social contribution that individuals make through their work. This insight is what animates arguments for legislating a living wage, for instance. In the nineteenth century, Pope Leo XII held that those who contribute to society through honest work deserve not whatever wage the market sets but a wage sufficient to satisfy basic needs. Responding to the new conditions of industrialism, where "workingmen have been given over, isolated and defenseless, to the callousness of employers and the greed of unrestrained competition," Pope Leo rejected the notion that the justice of wages is "fixed by free consent." Citing a "dictate of nature more imperious and more ancient than any bargain between man and man," Pope Leo held that every wage should be sufficient to "support the wage-earner in reasonable and frugal comfort."[9] In the United States, the living wage argument was extended to cover the support of the family. A family wage, argued Father John Ryan, was owed to any "laborer who complies in a reasonable degree with nature's law of work."[10] The case for a living wage has again found currency in recent years, especially in efforts focused on local governments.[11]

The idea underlying the living wage is that those who contribute to society—who comply with the "law of work"—deserve to share in the goods that social cooperation makes possible. Although subject to competing interpretations of what counts as "living," the case for a living wage involves a critique of the social fit. It is not enough for justice that people are successfully recruited to roles aligned with their skills and talents. Nor is it sufficient if the distribution of work maximizes the productivity. Justice requires that the interests of individuals count, and for this social fit is insufficient. Even when social fit is satisfied, some may give more than they get. This may be just in that it serves the common good, and yet be unjust in that those who contribute get less than they deserve. The living wage aims to bring these two sides into some alignment by asking that those who comply with the "law of work" make enough to live in good health, to sustain families, and to participate in the common life of the society.

For advocates of a living wage, a fit between aptitudes and tasks that maximizes contribution to social needs is insufficient to satisfy the demands of justice. Nor, as we will see, was social fit enough to satisfy Aristotle. In discussing one of the worst and most violent roles in Athens—slavery—Aristotle introduced an important modification of the standard of fit.[12] For Aristotle, it is not a sufficient justification to claim that society gets something important if some are forced to be slaves. For a role like slavery to be just, it must also be the case that the role is aligned with the best purposes of those who fill it. In this case, Aristotle asks not only for a social fit but also for a personal fit between persons and their work. Because justice, in Aristotle's argument, demands more than a social fit, Aristotle placed slavery under a severe burden of justification. Indeed, by raising the standard beyond social fit, he undermined his own effort to defend that role.

Aristotle and Personal Fit

Given that he did not take human beings to be moral equals in the first place, we might think Aristotle would not be troubled by slavery. After all, his ideal political regime—the regime we would pray for but cannot attain—contains slavery.[13] Moreover, the practice of slavery was useful, perhaps so useful as to seem necessary—not only to Athens but also to the virtues that Aristotle praised. As Bernard Williams claims about fifth-century Athenians, "No way of life was accessible that preserved what was worthwhile to them and did without slavery."[14] The citizen's practice of deliberation, and the cultivation of courage, friendship, and the other virtues of Aristotle's *Ethics* all required leisure. Yet because the working life precluded leisure and a broad education, it was irreconcilable with living a full and excellent life.[15] The good life for some required the oppression of others, for the good life needed leisure, which in turn required that others take care of the work—the growing, the mining, the caretaking and cleaning, the building and making—that living together generated. There seemed no way for all simultaneously to develop the virtues and share in excellence.

Any critique of slavery therefore would have to call into question not only slavery but also the life it supported, a life Aristotle endorsed. Indeed Aristotle defends slavery—but curiously, he defends slavery only of a sort, and not the sort practiced in Athens. His partial defense invokes not the social fit we saw in Plato's account but a kind of personal fit that gives more emphasis to what individuals deserve, independent of what they contribute. For slavery to be just, Aristotle argues, those who occupy the role must also fit it, meaning not only that the role equips those in it to contribute maximally to society, but also that the role develops their best capacities. To justify a role like slavery in terms of personal fit, the usefulness of the role must be complemented by its beneficial effect on those in it.

The justice of slavery thus depends on whether slaves find their best expression in the role. Aristotle ranks human capacities hierarchically: the physical capacities of movement and growth, for instance, are of a lower order than the intellectual capacities. Because slavery, as Aristotle sees it, demands the work of the body but not of the mind, it can be justified only if slaves are those for whom the "best that can come from them" is "the use of the body."[16] From the perspective of Plato's social fit, it would be enough if those with weaker intellectual capacities than others inhabited the role, for such a distribution of talent would be socially optimal. But Aristotle pointedly asks for more. He insists that slavery can be justified only if individual slaves develop the best capacities they contain, irrespective of social need. His hierarchical ranking of human capacities serves as a standard of judgment that is independent of social needs. Thus slavery requires persons in whom the intellectual capacities are not merely weak in comparison to others but are nearly absent. They are, in Aristotle's terms, "natural slaves," as different from others as "the soul from body or man from beast." For them, Aristotle claims, slavery would be a better condition than freedom. Although not established for the sake of slaves, slavery is, for them, "both advantageous and just."[17]

Here we see what irretrievably separates Aristotle's moral world from ours: he thought some human beings were in fact "slaves by nature," so limited that slavery, for them, would be an advantage.[18] Even on his own terms, this standard raises practical difficulties for Aristotle's defense. How beings of such limited intellect could in fact carry out their work—which involved more intellectual demands than Aristotle was prepared to recognize—renders the analysis nearly incoherent. Apart from this, another difficulty arises from his recognition that those who in fact were enslaved were not natural slaves. As Aristotle remarks, slaves came to their role not through some mechanism that efficiently picked out those with very limited capacities but rather through bad luck. Suffering defeat at war, for instance, is not, as Aristotle must concede, an accurate way of identifying those who fit the category of the natural slave. Therefore, according to the standard Aristotle imposes—personal fit—slavery was unjust.

This is why Aristotle notes that those who assert slavery to be unjust "are in a certain manner correct."[19] Yet having recognized something of slavery's injustice, Aristotle does not suggest the role might be eradicated, or even that its violence be ameliorated. For one, Aristotle's political theory was not aimed at reform. He did not suppose himself on a mission, uncovering the truth for the sake of remaking the world in its image; on the contrary, he had a keen appreciation of the world's resistance to good intentions.[20] And unlike moral philosophers who think their knowledge equips them to dictate to legislators, he admitted the partial autonomy of politics. Yet aside from his conservatism and philosophic modesty, Aristotle thought slavery a necessary injustice. To the extent that he saw slavery as an injustice—and to an extent he did—he did not see any way around it. Doing away with slavery or its functional equivalent would not have extended the good life to those who lacked it. As he saw it, either some must live like slaves so that others may transcend toil, or all must engage in toil and forsake any possibility of living well. The defense of slavery rests not on its justice but its social necessity.

Later defenders of slavery and oppressive work invoked a similar kind of necessity. For example, Bernard Mandeville's eighteenth-century argument against charity schools took this form. All luxury and comfort, Mandeville claimed, sit on a foundation of hard, mundane, dirty work. The advantages of leisure—comfort, education, sport, art, and science—depend on this foundation. But because such work is undesirable, because it does not fit well with human capacities and aspirations, it is avoided whenever it can be. "No Body will do the dirty slavish Work that can help it," Mandeville asserted. Therefore it is necessary, he argued, that politics "cultivate the Breed" of those so poor and ignorant that they cannot help but be grateful for even the worst work, for "if no body did want no body would work."[21]

American defenders of slavery offered a similar argument. For instance, unlike those defenses that claimed slaves did in fact fit their role, Senator James Henry Hammond's 1858 "mud-sill" speech looked to the social necessity of oppressive working conditions. In every society, he argued, "there must be a class to do mean duties, to perform the drudgeries of life," to make possible the relief from labor that civilization requires. Every society, he said, needs a class with "a lower order of intelligence and but little skill." He explained: "Such a class you must have, or you would not have that other class which leads progress, refinement, and civilization. It constitutes the very mud-sills of society and of political government; and you might as well attempt to build a house in the air, as to build either the one or the other, except on mud-sills." Hammond overlooked the issue of fit and focused on the social necessity that renders inevitable a class of "poor hardworking people, who support everybody, and starve themselves."[22]

For Hammond, as for Mandeville and Aristotle, part of the business of politics is to oppress. The oppression is not without a point, as they would describe it. It is necessary for the best things and the greatest human achievements: no oppression, no progress. Yet the category of personal fit shows us why the oppression, whatever it brings, is at the same time unjust. The problem is not only that workers on the bottom fail to give their full consent but also that the work is fundamentally misaligned with their capacities as human beings. It neither develops what is best in them nor facilitates their individuality nor serves their independent purposes; rather, it constrains and prohibits their development as human beings. Without the category of fit that Aristotle introduces in his discussion of slavery, the very problem at stake diminishes. With it, the problem is stark. And from it arises a dilemma: does the best that society is capable of require constraining some so they fill roles that neither they nor anyone can be said to fit?

For a nineteenth-century utopian socialist such as Charles Fourier, no such dilemma is inevitable, no injustice necessary. For each necessary task there is someone fit to carry it out. All work could be made attractive—to someone. Even "loathsome tasks that ordinary workers would find debasing," he says, like cleaning stables and slaughtering animals, would attract young children "who love to wallow in the mire and play with dirty things."[23] The expectation that social needs and individual fulfillment could be wholly harmonized is but one aspect of Fourier's utopianism. Like all modern socialists, Fourier placed his hope in the expectation that a social organization of work would radically increase productivity. And increasing productivity, more than anything else, is what would ameliorate the nasty trade-off that Aristotle and other preindustrial thinkers faced, where someone's advantage came at another's expense.

What was once seen as a necessary connection between oppression and progress has been immensely relaxed by the productive capacity of modern economies. The elixir of productivity growth, by which the vast enrichment of some corresponds to the moderate enrichment of all, does much to mitigate the grim social facts that Hammond, Mandeville, and Aristotle faced. At the same time, we have not completely escaped Aristotle's predicament. Advanced industrial economies also create a variety of necessary tasks, not all of which are good to perform; even with great advances in productivity, economic need itself remains a necessary spur to getting these jobs done. The promise of growth is that all can become wealthy together, yet still the profits of some are related to the low wages of others, as the resistance to increasing the minimum wage, the financial markets' celebration of layoff announcements, and the export of labor-intensive jobs abroad all testify. The legions of workers imported to work the fields that Americans are affluent enough to shun, to drive taxis and to stitch suburban clothes, all reveal something of the old logic of work. That such work is so useful as to seem necessary, while also so undesirable as to require economic necessity to prod people to do it, suggests that the regime of economic growth has not fully transcended the logic of work that Aristotle identified. The category of personal fit reminds us that whatever nominal consent people give, still the worst sort of work, to which no one seems "fitted," often needs compulsion.

Natural Identities

Aristotle's category of personal fit illuminates a particular kind of injustice, where some are constrained in order that others may thrive. Yet the category, in Aristotle's rendering, seems to depend on a strange assumption about human nature: it supposes that individuals have a highly specific and rather fixed natural identity. Individuals fit their roles, in this view, when natural identities and social roles align, as when the natural slaves are those who fill the social role of slaves. Ascriptive natural identities serve as the basis for a social hierarchy. As the "natural slave" is born to do the work of the body, so others are born to think, or to command, or to make: they ought to be the philosophers, the generals, the artisans. The modern affirmation of human equality rejects the notion that social inequality could ever have such a natural basis. Human beings are not marked by nature to fit one station in the hierarchy of social places: "The mass of mankind has not been born with saddles on their backs," Thomas Jefferson insisted, "nor a favored few booted and spurred, ready to ride them."[24] Natural identities and the inequality they presuppose thus seem fundamentally opposed to democratic equality.

Yet we might accept the idea of "natural identities" without mapping it onto any social hierarchy, and instead see it as the basis of individuality and social diversity. The idea of natural identity can even motivate egalitarian aims, as for instance in the way it informs a concept of alienation. For example, consider the experience of alienation as it appears in the film *Being John Malkovich,* in which a character who takes himself to be a puppeteer *by nature* tries to find his place in a world that will not employ him as a puppeteer, that offers no social space to accommodate his natural identity. The protagonist's natural identity has no social location; only the identity's residual skill (dexterity) has market value (he forsakes puppeteering for an office filing job). In the most radical extension of this, society suffocates our natural identity: to be human is to be alienated. In a less extreme way, this experience—possessing a nature society cannot accommodate—is recognizable enough. Often we feel that something in our nature cannot find its right expression in the social world; while this can make the world seem to be strange and radically at odds with who we are, still we must adapt ourselves so we can make our way in the world. This feeling of possessing a natural identity (disjoined from any corresponding assumptions of natural inequality) helps make sense of the experience that social roles and social constraints impede us from being who we are—when, in short, our roles do not fit us.

Yet it is one thing to conceive of oneself as a puppeteer, another to think that in some metaphysical or essential sense one *is* a puppeteer. Conceiving of fit as entailing a very specific natural identity leads to both exaggerating and understating human alienation. The more precisely we conceive of a natural identity, the more difficult it becomes to map the identity onto a social role, and the more extensively (and exaggeratedly) we perceive our alienation. To think that for every social role there is a "natural fit" (as if there might be natural systems analysts, welders, window washers, or grocery baggers) makes much of worldly life and perhaps all of the working life seem alienating. Perhaps there is some truth in this extreme picture of alienation, but practically, the effect of casting human alienation so broadly undercuts the critical leverage a concept like alienation might possess, and at the same time it misconceives what it means to fit a role.

To imagine that we might conform so exquisitely with the social world makes social roles seem more fixed than they actually are. Social roles are in flux—they differ in industrial, postindustrial, and agrarian economies. There is no reason to suppose that the natural identities we might possess should change across time and space to accommodate particular economic systems. That individuals might be imprinted by nature with specific job descriptions thus imposes an absurd degree of coherence on human nature and the social world. No one is a puppeteer *by nature* in the sense that he was "made" to play with puppets. Puppetry is a social practice, invented by human beings, with standards specific to it that are sustained by human beings. Neither it nor other roles that entail a division of labor are natural categories merely awaiting the individuals designed for them.

Capacities and Fit

The idea of fit is better conceived without assuming that people have some specific natural identity that society might accommodate or frustrate. Indeed, aside from his curious claim about natural slaves, even Aristotle does not suppose there might be natural identities that align with every job. He does not imagine there could be natural shoemakers, for instance, nor that there ought to be for shoemaking to be justified.[25] More to the point for Aristotle—even in his assessment of slavery—is the general relationship between capacities and roles. In the *Politics,* Aristotle singles out only several human capacities: physical growth, desire or appetite, and reason. These capacities generate claims. Reason, he claims, enjoys a natural superiority to the other capacities; as such, it ought to guide and constrain their exercise. The ideal relationship between reason and the passions is the subject of the *Ethics,* in which the virtues (courage, generosity, pride, justice, and so on) describe the ways reason and passion might best cooperate in action. Yet this ideal relationship eludes most; either badly habituated or lacking in an authoritative rational capacity, they act out of passion in ways destructive to others. In Aristotle's *Politics* this comes to be the decisive fact that governs the allocation of social roles. Those roles that most require reason ought to be filled by those who most completely possess it. In this way, Aristotle's hierarchical conception of human nature corresponds to an aristocratic politics, where some are coerced to occupy roles that "fit" them regardless of what they would choose.

The trouble for Aristotle was that a seemingly necessary role—slavery—both required reason and insulted it. The condition of slavery stunts the capacities of those who do not fit the role and precludes living a life defined by its own ends. Thus he said it would be better if necessary tasks were done automatically—if "the shuttles would weave themselves." But in fact these tasks required self-directing human beings, capable at least of understanding and executing directions. While one completely bereft of reason is incapable of doing the slave's work, possessing reason renders him unworthy of the conditions such work imposes. Aristotle tries to find his way out of this problem by positing an incoherent kind of being, one who shares in human traits enough to carry out tasks yet is so lacking in rational capacity as to be inhuman.

These are difficulties Aristotle creates for himself by invoking the standard of fit, which turns out to be a profoundly critical standard. Only the fact that Aristotle identifies the human soul as something independent of society—grounded in human nature, which consists of various capacities that generate their own claims—allows him to conceive that a socially beneficial division of labor is also unjust. Without such a standard rooted in an individual's claims independent of society, he could not have located any basis for questioning the system of social fit in which society's tasks are optimally carried out. At its core, personal fit is not about natural identities but general human capacities and the claims they generate. The basic insight is that individuals deserve something simply by virtue of the capacities they bear. In particular, they deserve that these capacities be cultivated and facilitated rather than thwarted and suffocated by the roles society offers.

This basic insight is in no way specific to an aristocratic worldview, and is available—and indeed in some sense supports—in the liberal and democratic affirmation of human equality. This affirmation does not say that human beings are identical (and that therefore any variation in their roles or social condition is unjust) but rather that each has a claim justice cannot overlook. To be sure, the democratic perspective is less discriminating than the aristocratic, for it distributes the claim to rule more broadly and thus elevates the capacities of self-direction and self-expression, feeling, and imagination, along with reason. But it cannot do without the basic insight that our capacities generate claims, and that this has moral consequences for the sorts of social roles that we take to be fitting.

This insight, for instance, characterizes Martha Nussbaum's discussion of human functioning. Broadly following Aristotle, Nussbaum singles out a variety of facts and capacities that define the "human form of life": mortality, bodily necessity, sensation, cognition, infant development, practical reason, affiliation, relatedness, play, and separateness.[26] These involve "certain functional capacities at which societies should aim for their citizens." Together they establish a minimal threshold, for without their satisfaction life "will be lacking in humanness."[27] They point to a minimal threshold of fit that applies to human beings in general and affirms that each, from the richest to the poorest, "hath a life to live."[28] Following this approach, the category of fit can be used to assess whether a role gives so little space to elemental human capacities that it fails to fit human beings in general. This is what Aristotle showed about slavery, and it is also what many claim about contemporary sweatshop work. Other roles, too, might so deform our humanity by stunting basic human capacities that, when considered from the perspective of fit, we conclude they ought to be abolished if at all possible. Insofar as they are so useful or necessary as to make eradication seem impossible, the basic standard of fit nonetheless shows them to be unjust. They offer less than any human being deserves. In such cases, the standard of fit asks that we consider some way of ameliorating the injustice, such as sharing the role or restructuring it. This minimal standard of fit is the subject of the next chapter, which investigates the problem of service work.

Beyond issuing in a minimum threshold, an account of human capacities also points to a more ideal standard of fulfillment. It is one thing to satisfy those basic functions that define a human form of life but another to fully exercise the most distinctive or most cherished human capacities. Work that meets this more exalted standard is not merely acceptable but fulfilling; it is not a regrettable necessity so much as a good thing in itself, worthy in its own right of some devotion. All ideals, even the ideal of freedom, privilege certain capacities over others. Freedom particularly elevates the capacity to choose, the act through which, as John Stuart Mill says, all the other human capacities come into focus. We care about choice, for instance, in part because we think individuals are best positioned to decide for themselves what best fits them; but we care about choice also because we hope people will decide well, that they will find and decide on roles that fit them.[29] A world of choice makes fitting work more relevant rather than less, at least for those who find themselves with some latitude in their decisions. Moreover, we might care that more people have more latitude in their choices from a conviction that the social world can offer some roles that are especially fitting, and that this is the basis for a worthwhile and satisfying life. In this way, consent and fit work together—each gives the other more urgency. The possibility of an excellent or optimal fit that goes well beyond a minimal threshold of generic humanness will be the subject of Chapters 5 through 8.

4

The Strains of Service

While the ancients applied the category of fit to an aristocratic order in which each was said to fit his or her fixed place, at the core of the concept of fit is an idea that affirms the liberal and democratic faith in moral individuality: each, by virtue of the capacities he or she bears, has a claim that justice cannot overlook. At root, this is what caused Aristotle such difficulty in defending slavery. The conviction that distinctively human capacities are held in general (as opposed to remaining the exclusive possession of some) at once rules out the possibility of "natural slaves" and gives humanity its moral standing. It is also what makes the category of fit available to a democratic age. The democratic interpretation of fit goes farther than insisting that each has a claim to a "human form of life," at least if this is understood only in the barest sense. As it rejects the idea that anyone could entirely *belong to* another, so it holds that each person has a claim to a life that in some sense can be said to be his or her *own*. Thus, justice must be concerned with what each deserves and cannot tolerate arrangements where some are used simply for the sake of others. One finds this familiar notion in one form or another in writings of the Levellers, Locke, Kant, and contemporary liberals.[1] To say that fit has a democratic interpretation is to acknowledge that the concept of fit must take stock of substantive conceptions about human equality and what it means to live decently or well that are independent of fit itself. That these ideas are not the same in every age or every regime does not mean that they are relativist in some deep sense.

Chief among these ideas in liberal democracy is the belief that each "has a life to live," with the consequence that no one ought to be forced by need or circumstance to live wholly for others. If this concept is rooted in our pride, it also reflects what we take to be a moral truth about the equal standing of human beings. A demanding but not utopian standard, it does not mean that each lives only for himself and that none can ever justly serve another. Rather it holds that fitting work, at the most basic level, equips each to live his or her own life, animated by its own projects and purposes. The burden that this democratic understanding of fit places on work roles comes into particular focus in domestic service, where one person tends to the personal needs of others. Insofar as this work is unbounded, it is in tension with the self-respect that democracies admirably nourish, and it violates what democratic citizens take themselves to be fitted to. In such cases, as this chapter will show, the category of fit asks that work at least be limited or bounded. As we will see in the case of domestic service, this notion is what informs the most basic understanding of fit in a democratic age.

By the late nineteenth century in America, domestic service ran headlong into the belief that no one is fitted to live a life composed entirely of service to others. Because such work engaged more women than any other single occupation of the time, the "problem" of domestic service received more attention and debate in women's magazines than any other subject between 1870 and 1920.[2] Lucy Maynard Salmon called domestic service the "great American question"; more than a question, Catharine Beecher and Harriet Beecher Stowe asserted, domestic service was "the great problem of life here in America."[3]

What problem did domestic service pose for nineteenth-century Americans? One might cast it as simply economic: middle-class women seeking domestic help could not attract enough servants, or reliable enough servants, at the wages they could afford or were willing to pay. But beneath this was a deeper issue: employers felt that they were *worthy* of service—that their needs were worthy enough to command the full-time service of others, even at the cost of displacing the independent needs of those performing the service. Prior to the advent of household technology, servants were necessary to a middle-class life. Yet potential servants, faced with the increasing range of employment options in the growing economy, asserted the elemental independence of their own lives: they took other jobs. A Maine housewife with five children and at the limit of her budget, for instance, complained that she was consistently outbid by neighboring mills.[4] Many refused work in domestic service even when it paid more than the mills; other servants simply quit— with a frequency that alarmed employers—often to accept the same job in a different household.[5] The resistance to domestic servitude was aimed not simply at low wages but at the definition of the job role itself, which did not fit the most basic assumptions of democratic citizens. The scope of the job was tyrannical; it enveloped the lives of those in it, and displaced their own ends in favor of the ends of those they served.

That servants, by the late nineteenth century, were *not* coerced offered them an important protection and certainly made the job better than it otherwise would be. But neither the logic of consent nor the action of giving and withholding consent can describe the nature of the service problem. The problem with the role had less to do with the circumstances of its acceptance than with something intrinsic to the job role itself: by fully dominating the lives of those inhabiting it, it could not give elemental scope to the independent ends or purposes of those in it. For their part, nineteenth-century critics and reformers suggested ways of both restructuring the role of domestic service and eliminating it. The subsequent introduction of household technology largely obviated the demand for domestic servants, rendering the "great American problem" a matter of less importance. Yet the general problem of assessing work roles that are at once socially needed and, if not only undesirable, also unjust, remains—albeit in different guises.

Indentures and the Claims of Consent

Consent is a signal that we find something acceptable. But when the only options are accepting or quitting, when one is precluded from shaping the condition one consents to, consent is a clumsy and inexact form of expression. Nonetheless, the fact that nineteenth-century servants worked only by their own consent and possessed the right of exit was a significant development, the result of achievements in the United States around the time of the American Revolution. Until then, many servants had been redemptioners, convicts sentenced to work in the colonies, or apprentices. All were bound to work in homes for a fixed period, either to pay off the cost of their passage to North America or to acquire a degree of training and maturity before working on their own. Other servants were without indenture but were still bound by law to serve a fixed tenure, which varied according to the age at which they began service.[6] To impede servants who tried to escape their bondage, various laws penalized those who harbored runaway servants, offered rewards for their return, and prohibited trading or bartering with servants. Such legal attempts at enforcing bondage were not wholly successful, for amid cheap and abundant open land, the difficulty of retaining servants who were similar in appearance to free men and women was great. The motives to run away were obvious for some: in Connecticut, masters could punish disobedient servants with up to "ten stripes" per offense. The punishment for runaways could also be severe—for instance, North Carolina constables were authorized to punish runaways with "as many lashes as the justice of the peace should see fit," not to exceed thirty-nine, "well laid on, on the Back of such Runaway." The plight of colonial indentured servants could be trying: "Oh," one wailed, "that you did see my daily and hourly sighs, groans, tears, and thumps that I afford my own breast, and rue and curse the time of my birth with holy Job."[7] For servants like these, the right of exit was not merely symbolic or nominal. For those impelled to make use of it, the right of exit constituted a fundamental and real distinction between free laborers and slaves.

Even without the right of exit, consent was critical to justifying colonial indenture. Except for convicts, indentured servants did consent to their indenture or bondage. Concerned about reports that people were being kidnapped and forced into indentured service, the British Committee for Foreign Plantations took measures in the seventeenth century to ensure that only people who voluntarily consented would become indentured servants.[8] To the extent that such measures were effective, they would have established that servants had consented to their condition at one moment in time. However, the nature of bondage even for a limited period means that this consent would not be continuous or durable, because few would give enduring consent to servitude. Was the discrete or momentary consent given by prospective indentures sufficient to justify their obligation to serve?

In some cases, discrete consent seems sufficient to generate obligation. People who voluntarily take on a loan, for instance, consent at one moment in time to take on an enduring obligation. Indentured servants are on this view more like homeowners paying off a mortgage than like slaves. Temporary servitude was the price of their support and passage to the New World, and they could no more quit their servitude and enjoy their place in the New World than the borrower could stop making monthly payments and yet keep the house. Only by discrete rather than continuous consent can individuals reliably take on future obligations in exchange for a form of advance payment. In essence, discrete consent is like making a promise—although given in one moment, the obligation it generates endures. That the consent involved in indentured service is momentary is not sufficient to hold that indentured service is unjust.

Rather than deriving from the discrete nature of consent, any injustice in indentured servitude must be rooted more directly in some substantive aspect of the contract itself. For a role that is voluntarily accepted to be unjust, there must be some limit on what even free people can agree to, some constraint on the condition in which persons can voluntarily place themselves. Before considering limits on what even free consent can justify, it is necessary to examine whether the consent that prospective indentures gave was free in the way necessary to confer any moral standing on the resulting contract. People, it might be argued, could be attracted to the "deal" that indentured servitude presented only if they were in a very desperate situation, and this desperation undermined the free nature of consent. Instead of an act of affirmation, the consent involved in indentured service was an act of resignation to the necessities of survival. As both an objective condition referring to the close proximity of starvation or hopelessness and a subjective condition relating to one's sense of this proximity, desperation undercuts freedom by compelling people—psychologically, if not by literal physical force—to accept whatever they can get in exchange for whatever they can give. Contracts made out of desperation, on this argument, are not free in the relevant moral sense, even if the desperate have given their express consent.

But to reject all contracts made when one party acts out of desperation would exclude too much. The concern about consenting out of desperation is always related to what it is that is consented to. While some might consent out of a sense of desperation to indentured servitude, others might consent to be bakers, car dealers, or lawyers. Some desperate people may get better deals than others. To hold that any contract is unjust when one party acts out of desperation would exclude even those cases in which one consents to perform work that is clean, safe, thoughtful, and remunerative. Any specific injustice in something like indentured servitude must depend not solely on the desperation of one of the parties but instead on something else about what specifically was agreed to. Desperation is objectionable only when it is combined with something else that is objectionable about the job itself.

In the case of indentured service, the injustice does have to do with ceding the right of exit, but the injustice does not derive simply from flawed aspects of consent. The injustice rather resides in the kind of dependence indentured service involves. Performing a job should not be treated like repaying a loan, for this would invest employers with commanding power while subjecting workers to abject dependence. To be in someone's employ, as opposed to being self-employed, always involves some dependence; insofar as wages are used to meet necessary expenses, the employee is dependent on the employer (and employers themselves may be very dependent on their workers). Although avoiding dependence has long motivated the American dream of self-employment, in a commercial society, almost no one is truly independent.[9] The right of exit is crucial to constraining the power of employers. It places a limit on the degree of dependence workers might be subject to. Without the right of exit, the authority of an employer can become the unlimited authority of a master.

What was unjust about indentured servitude, on this view, was that indentured servants had not only bosses who directed them in their tasks but masters who could exercise control over nearly every aspect of their life. With little legal recourse, stripped of the rights to travel, trade, and enter into contracts of their own making, indentured servants were subject to an unrestrained power. The master's authority, while not legally unlimited, was in fact extensive. For instance, although the law restricted for what causes and with what severity masters could punish servants, it did allow masters to use corporal punishment with disobedient servants. Denying the right of exit meant that servants could do nothing but submit. The mere fact of desperation is not sufficient to show that work is unjust. Rather, the objection is to the arbitrary power that people, from a sense of desperation, will be impelled to accept. Not even desperation makes certain conditions worthy of agreement. Although the case of indentured servitude points to the importance of a right of exit as one of the most basic elements of just work, it also leaves us a crucial question: is formal consent to a job, combined with the right of exit, sufficient to establish the justice of work? The case of voluntary domestic service reveals the importance of assessing job roles in terms of fit even when the right of exit is assured.

"Equality Makes New Men"

In an astute assessment of American master-servant relations, Alexis de Tocqueville examined whether contractual equality was sufficient to justify the actual inequality between masters and servants. Tocqueville contended that democratic equality deprived master-servant relations of the sort of justification that could allow masters and servants to think they naturally fit their roles. At the same time, he suggested, the moral force of the contract could justify by convention what could not be justified by the language of fit. The self-understandings that contractual relations nourish reconciled, on Tocqueville's view, the "actual inequality" of masters and servants with the "fancied equality between them."[10]

In contrast to the exclusively contractual relations between master and servant in America, Tocqueville notes, a deeper bond relates master and servant in aristocracy. A general awareness of hierarchical rank combines with the force of "long-shared memories" to form a bond between master and servant that overpowers differences in "fortune, education, opinion, and rights."[11] This bond is expressed in the master's enlarged sense of self and the servant's self-renunciation. At the "extreme," servants lose themselves in their master's identity and in turn the master takes an interest in the fate of his servants as if they were a part of him. By inculcating the belief that one is born into a class in which one must remain and by supporting within each class distinct "conceptions of right and wrong," the social conditions of aristocracy create a belief in a "fixed order" of society. Master and servant come to have "no natural resemblance."[12] Natural difference rises above mere distinction and assumes the proportion of a difference in rank, so that actual inequality becomes the mirror of their natural difference. What cements the bond between master and servant is the sense that each is naturally fit to a different rank, and the respective ranks are linked by reference to a larger hierarchical order.

The aristocratic order casts servants as lower, less complete, and less perfect than the nobles they serve. Inadequate alone, servants find their completion through their service. By placing themselves at the service of someone higher and taking part in their master's identity, they share in his excellence and nobility. Therefore, their self-sacrifice is for the sake of something better. Were the master not superior, if the master's soul could not complete their own, the servants' sacrifice would be pointless, absurd, and unjustifiable. But in the master's greatness the servants find their completion, or receive their due in their station. And conversely, because of the master's nobility, he deserves the service of servants.

This understanding of the relation between master and servants, which Tocqueville calls "both touching and ridiculous," is impossible for Americans even to imagine, he says. The conceptual impasse stems from the transformed status of both master and servant under democratic equality. "Equality," Tocqueville writes, "makes new men of the servant and of the master and establishes new connections between them." As "new men" standing in relation to each other, the servant is "in some fashion" the equal of the master. No natural inferiority or superiority between them is recognized. Yet if both master and servant are equal, then what determines— and what could justify—the fact that one gives orders and the other obeys? The right to rule and the duty to obey, Tocqueville claims, result from "[a] temporary and freely made agreement." The further question about why one can consent to command while the other must agree to obey is decided, Tocqueville indicates, not by respective station in a fixed hierarchy but by *accident:* wealth and poverty, power and obedience, "accidentally put great distances between two men," Tocqueville observes. Master and servant could change places, and indeed, Tocqueville says, most servants would prefer to exchange lots. Even in their own minds both master and servant know that they are not suited to their roles by virtue of "some profound difference" between them.[13] On Tocqueville's description, the justice of consent displaces the justice of fit.

Moreover, Tocqueville claims, equality places the master-servant relationship on stable footing. The master and servant can "look at each other without pride or humility" because the contract that establishes the basis for authority and obedience also marks their limits. The master's power becomes limited; he becomes an employer whose authority is restricted to the job site; beyond the radius of his command, "they are two citizens, two men," Tocqueville writes. As a soldier takes orders from his commander in the army but is the equal of his commander in civil life, so master and servant stand on equal footing outside the boundaries of the job.[14] By restricting the scope of lived inequality, contractual equality makes stable obedience possible. "In a democracy," Tocqueville says, "there is nothing degrading about the status of a domestic servant, because it is freely adopted and temporary and because it is not stigmatized by public opinion and creates no permanent inequality between master and servant." But master-servant relations are not so benign, Tocqueville states, when amid democratic social conditions aristocratic prejudices persist. Masters then fail to see themselves as the accidental repositories of limited authority and instead conceive that they are naturally superior to those who serve them. Meanwhile, servants (who no longer share aristocratic self-understandings) fail to grasp the justice of contractual equality and therefore also miss how democratic equality is consistent with obedience. With such misunderstandings, a house, like the larger political world, is riven by "permanently suspicious rival powers."[15]

This image of domestic discord, with only a bit of exaggeration, is an apt description of late nineteenth-century domestic service in America. In the eyes of many servants, formal equality of contract was not sufficient to lend domestic service the dignity Tocqueville described. This was due in part, as Tocqueville speculated, to enduring aristocratic prejudices on the part of employers. But it also stemmed from the incapacity of free contracts to completely displace the justice of fit. Democratic understandings do not dissolve the justice of fit so much as they reshape it. To fit one's job comes to mean, in the most basic and elemental sense, that the job serves one's own purposes. This service to the worker's own purposes may be more or less direct; it may have more to do with what the job provides (security, support, comfort) than what it is or what it intrinsically expresses. This link to the worker's own purposes depends on more than consent; independent of consent, democratic fit demands something of the conditions of work.

To understand how a concern with fit persisted even amid the contractual equality of master and servant in nineteenth-century America, it is necessary to go beyond Tocqueville's analysis and attend to the lived experience of nineteenth-century American servants, as reported by both servants and their employers. Women in domestic service often did not believe they were suited to the job of serving others, and this lack of fit was exacerbated by the fact that the job crowded out activities that might be pursued outside of work. The way the job consumed all the energies of servants made the lack of fit more apparent and a persistent source of frustration.

Actual Inequality amid Contractual Equality

In the lived experience of late nineteenth-century American servants, the actual inequality of employer and servant overshadowed their status as contractual equals. Around midcentury, Americans with servants began to take steps that would clearly segregate and differentiate themselves from the women who lived and worked in their homes. Backdoor servants' entrances, hidden from public view, began to be used in American homes. The layout of rooms was designed to make servants as invisible as possible: back stairways and halls allowed servants to move about as they were working without entering the family's living area. Sliding doors and pantries separated dining rooms from kitchens, and kitchens, where the "help" once worked and ate side-by-side with their employers, became a workplace reserved for servants alone, where they prepared the meals they served to the family in a separate dining room.[16] Middle- and upper-class Americans expected servants to be present but inconspicuous. When overhearing conversations among the family, a servant was expected never to contribute to or participate in them. The ideal servant, according to one housekeeping guide, would never even be caught "listening to what is said at the table, instead of concentrating attention upon the waiting."[17] Good servants, in short, attended to the family's needs but presented none of their own.

Physical separation and quiet habits made servants less conspicuous, but—except where some servants in large households never entered the family area—it was impossible for them to be completely invisible. Nor would employers necessarily have wanted this, for it would have precluded that visible deference that some employers thought appropriate. More Americans, for example, decided to have their servants wear uniforms, or livery, lest they be "mistaken for a member of the family."[18] Visible deference in this form could help prevent this mistake's being made not only by outsiders but also by the servants and the family itself. The subservient manners and appearance of servants could help support a family's sense of generalized superiority. This feeling of superiority might be important for those who had given part of themselves over to the pleasures of domination. But even more crucial, a sense of superiority could help a family justify the fact that it was being served, and combat the notion that the servants themselves might need servants. Habits of subservience and segregated entrances and workspaces symbolized a general inferiority by virtue of which servants were thought not to need or deserve the same attention to their health, the same rest, or the same leisure as the families they served.

This measure of visible deference and subservience also established for servants that they worked *for* the family but were not members *of* it. When servants who were addressed by their first name were expected to use proper last names when addressing family members, when they wore distinguishing uniforms and practiced habits of obedience, they were reminded that their place was in the house but not in the family. As one mistress told a servant who objected to wearing livery, "You must remember that if you take a servant's place you have to accept the limitations of a servant."[19] Those limitations, in addition to meeting the responsibility for housework, included serious restrictions on social lives and personal freedom. Servants had little if any time off from work, and many employers made it their business to supervise whatever social life their servants were able to manage. As one servant wrote, "Our employer feels, somehow, that she is our guardian and has the right to supervise all comings and outgoings, to question us about what we do in our leisure, and to be 'mistress' as well as employer."[20] Most servants, of course, had precious little leisure, and they usually lacked a space in which to entertain company in the house. Some employers discouraged visits even by relatives.[21]

Because servants spent their days and nights in a home where they did not belong, because they could not share in the very advantages of home life that they helped create, they often felt an oppressive isolation and loneliness. "Ladies wonder how their girls can complain of loneliness in a house full of people," one servant told Lucy Salmon, "but Oh! it is the worst kind of loneliness; their share is but the work of a house, they do not share in the pleasures and delight of a home. One must remember," the servant continued, "that there is a difference between a house, a place of shelter, and a home, a place where all your affections are centered."[22] Lacking the time and freedom for an independent social life, and also excluded from the communal life—the meals, discussions, and family outings—of the home they served, servants could build no identity outside their role as servants. Further, they were denied social recognition even in their role as servants. Outside the house, this lack of recognition increased the already great social distance between servants and their employers. It is "an understood thing," one employer said, "that the lady and the girl do not know each other outside."[23]

Could nineteenth-century employers have adopted more democratic manners toward servants? Recognition, real affection, and respect, after all, are possible even toward those who serve us. Some employers thought that adopting a more democratic posture toward servants would undermine the role—that once recognized socially, servants would no longer be willing to serve; they might no longer tolerate and accept what Tocqueville called the "actual inequality" defining their relationship to their employers. Among these employers, the denial of social recognition was no mere oversight or pointless act of snobbery. Rather, it was a calculated action designed to impress upon servants their proper station. "I think that many women would be more kind and friendly," an employer said, "but it spoils the girls, and gives them false notions about their place."[24]

The severely long hours that household servants worked exacerbated the problems of subservience, denial of social recognition, and loss of personal freedom. The most common complaints servants made about their jobs centered on the length of the working day. Many worked a ten-hour day at the least, and some worked up to fourteen hours a day, six or seven days of the week.[25] One 1898 study of Massachusetts domestic servants revealed that about one hour and forty minutes per day was spent responding to employers' spontaneous requests, increasing the working day to more than thirteen hours. All told, between tending to regular chores and responding to employers' calls, servants often had no free time at all. Scheduled time off was scarce as well. Before 1870, servants customarily were given just one afternoon or evening off every two weeks; at the turn of the century, the custom was part of Sunday and one evening each week.[26]

Most servants considered this insufficient. One, noting that her employer provided her with a comfortable and attractive bedroom, claimed that she would gladly give the room up in exchange for "a little time to myself." Her employer would "sit in her sitting room on the second floor and ring for me twenty times a day to do little things, and she wanted me up till eleven to answer the bell, for she had a great deal of company." With no time during her waking hours to rest, she said, "I was all worn out and at last I had to go."[27] On their feet most of the day, with scant opportunity to relax, servants complained of the sheer fatigue their jobs induced. One well-off woman who worked as a servant as an experiment and reported on her experience said she felt the onset of physical breakdown after working only six weeks: "Instead of toughening I was breaking; each week I lost something that I did not regain."[28] Even the working-hours restrictions passed by state legislatures failed to address the situation of domestic servants. Forty-six states and the District of Columbia passed legislation between 1858 and 1921 restricting the conditions or hours of work for women, yet all the laws excluded work performed in private homes.[29]

The net effect of the long hours, hard work, isolation, low social status, and loss of personal liberty was that many working women tried to avoid becoming a servant if at all possible. Where it was available, many chose factory work instead. At least in the factory "you know when you are done," one woman said.[30] Explaining why she preferred retail work to domestic service, another woman said, "Often I could forget the shop altogether for a time, while as a servant my home was a few hard chairs and two soiled quilts. My every hour was sold, night and day. I had to be constantly in the presence of people who looked down upon me as an inferior."[31] A former servant explained, "It's hard to give up your whole life to somebody else's orders, and always feel as if you were looked at over a wall like; but so it is, and you won't get girls to try it, 'til somehow or other things are different."[32] This sense—that domestic service could not meet the elementary expectations of democratic citizens to live a life centered on their own purposes and projects—was what motivated the servant problem. The contractual equality between servant and mistress was insufficient to lend the dignity to the servant role that would have made it attractive. Neither contractual equality nor the fact of consent could square servants' lived experience with their sense of pride.

Living for Others

The problem with domestic service had to do with the shape of the job itself rather than the circumstances of its acceptance, as indicated by the resistance of domestic servants to being called servants. Lillian Pettengill, who, after graduating from college spent two years working as a servant in Philadelphia, asserted, "A domestic tradeswoman I am, a chambermaid, a waitress, an employee with an employer, but a servant with a mistress—never. I am an American."[33] Such resistance to a mere label—and an accurate one at that—seemed foolish and sentimental to employers. Against the tendency to call servants "the help," James Fenimore Cooper argued that this obscured the reality of the role. "They who aid their masters in the toil may be deemed 'helps,' but they who perform all the labor do not assist, or help to do the thing, but they do it themselves . . . In all cases in which the people of America have retained the *things* of their ancestors," he said, "they should not be ashamed to keep the *names*."[34] The very persistence and depth of workers' objection to the name *servant,* as well as the strenuous objection by some employers to changing it, suggests that something more than a mere word was at stake in the disagreement. Part of servants' objection to the word was due to the historical and etymological roots of servants in servitude and slavery, but the resistance was also motivated by an objection to the role itself. This explains why the debate over the word *servant* called forth such energy and conviction: changing the name was simple—transforming the role itself would have been a far more difficult matter.

No single aspect of the role when viewed in isolation shows what was objectionable: loneliness, isolation, overbearing bosses, and long hours were and are common to many other jobs. Rather, the problem with the servant role was that all the separate objects of complaint combined to form a role that subsumed the servant's identity and almost wholly displaced her independent purposes and projects. The job prevented those doing it from taking on or pursuing any purposes of their own, and the conditions of democratic equality make it difficult to claim that anyone is suited to a role that involves living wholly for another's purposes. Servants felt as if they were simply being used. Although they did not exist for the sake of another in the extreme Lockean sense that their preservation was at the disposal of another, there is an important respect in which servants did exist only for the sake of others.

Servants' work offered neither the sort of "internal goods" nor the kinds of external goods necessary to adequately acknowledge that they possessed their own ends and in some sense deserved to live for themselves (Chapter 8 will examine internal goods more extensively). Internal goods are habits of the mind, heart, and body that are instilled through participating in certain activities. They might include the grace that comes to dancers, the intuition of a mechanic, the manners and sociability of a waiter. They are distinct from external goods such as money, status, and power in two ways: first, they are internal to us—they are "goods of the soul." Second, they can be gained only through engagement in an activity. They cannot be borrowed or purchased, nor can their value be realized by merely simulating them. At their best, internal goods are valuable not only with respect to the activity in which they originate but also, in small and large ways, they assist in life more generally.[35] The ability to gain the internal goods that an activity offers is what equips us to "fit" an activity; in this respect, internal goods demand something of us.

Defenders of domestic service occasionally tried to defend the role in terms of its internal goods. The work was said, for instance, to serve an educative function—some claimed that servants would learn housekeeping and would eventually be able to apply that learning in homes of their own. Perhaps some servants were in fact committed to housework and hoped to acquire some valuable practice in the job, yet most, whatever the rewards of keeping one's own home, did not identify their own purposes with working in others' homes. Domestic work—cut off from the home and family life that such work supported—could not support any sense among servants that they belonged in the role. Servants worked not for their own purposes but for the purposes of those whom they served. This was the sense in which servants existed only for others' use.

Where work offers no internal reward, the external rewards become that much more important. Servants did of course earn, but their severe hours precluded them from shaping much of a life of their own outside of work. Living on the job site with scarcely any time off, servants had no time for their own pursuits, such as their own family. Some free time is essential so workers can rest or replenish themselves, if only to go back to work. Where there are few or no internal rewards to be realized through work, free time becomes crucial in order that workers find the space to pursue their own activities and projects. Some space for leisure in addition to rest—that is, free time for the sake of pursuing intrinsically rewarding practices—is necessary if people are to partake at all in distinctly human ends. Marx criticized capitalism because, he said, the worker "is at home when he is not working, and when he is working, is not at home."[36] Denied independent social recognition and the time necessary to devote themselves to their own lives, servants became dominated by an occupational role that could offer no intrinsic purpose and no space for purposes located outside of work.

Democratic equality does not replace the justice of fit; it changes what it means to fit one's work. For democratic citizens who are taken as moral equals, fit with work means locating one's own purposes in one's work or enabling one's purposes through work. Amid the democratic self-understandings of nineteenth-century America, servants and some employers sensed that few if indeed any were fit simply to serve. Women in America, both immigrant and native, felt they could not adequately serve their own ends while existing only to obey another's command and tend to the personal needs of their employer.

A few realized that the conditions and ideals of democratic equality could not make sense of how one might fit a life of only service. As one employer said, "In a country whose battle cry is equality, there is no such thing as a good servant class." Said another, "Servants are born, not made, and America does not furnish the environment conducive to such birth."[37] Equality brings out the moral problem with servant work, but not simply because a belief in equality engenders such pride that people are unwilling to serve others. Democratic pride decreases obsequious manners, but this, by itself, does not undermine service as such. More than manners, what democratic equality calls into question is the notion that one person's life should be lived for the sake of another. By contrast, Tocqueville's analysis suggests how aristocratic arrangements make it possible for the servant to take part in the master's life. Servants could accept the master's purposes, Tocqueville contends, because they could vicariously find an intrinsic purpose through their work. Democratic equality, however, challenges the idea that anyone's soul is so incomplete that he can find his purpose only by serving another's. Where even the poorest "hath a life to live, as the greatest,"[38] each person's life is supposed to have its own purpose. Democratic equality precludes the existence of a "good servant class."

Reforming Service Work

Understanding what was wrong with domestic service does not by itself address the larger problem nineteenth-century Americans faced. Domestic servants were essential to American middle-class life. They enabled middle-class women to devote themselves to social and religious concerns and men to business careers and political pursuits. Yet as useful as servants were, the persistence of the servant problem made it clear that few if any could think of themselves as suited to the work. People considered a variety of solutions, which can be grouped in several broad categories: abolishing the

role, either through a technological fix or by promoting self-reliance; distributing the work more equally, by rotation or draft; or
reforming the role, perhaps by attending to conditions like hours
and pay.

At the less practical extreme, Edward Bellamy described a utopian vision of a servantless society in his book *Looking Backward*.
No servants would be necessary in the socialist society of the future,
he claimed. By varying the hours worked and the honor attached to
different occupational roles, all jobs would be rendered equally attractive. All the domestic servants society needed would be supplied—that is, Bellamy pointed out, if a society of social equals
would need servants at all. With public laundries, collective kitchens, electricity, and labor-saving inventions, servants would more
likely be rendered superfluous.[39] The implicit suggestion in a society
where private housework is abolished is that domestic service as
traditionally conceived could never be squared with democratic
equality and could never be rendered as attractive as other roles.

The idea that service work somehow needs to be abolished in a
democracy is also reflected in the down-to-earth admiration Harriet
Beecher Stowe expressed for the "lady who does her own work."
Even "ladies"—that is, women "of education, cultivation, and refinement, of liberal tastes and ideas"—could perform household
chores without help, Stowe claimed. In fact, she said, they would
carry out housework with expert efficiency and pare every task to
its essential minimum. Frugal, systematic, and in calm control of
every detail of house life, they would also raise their children to be
industrious and, more crucial, independent. The apparent necessity
of servants, according to Stowe, was rooted in the laziness endemic
in human nature and a misguided desire to impress cosmopolitan
visitors. Although Stowe conceded that the demand for servants
would persist whatever the merits of doing one's own work, even
those who employed servants would be better off for having at
some point done their household work themselves. For only then
could they say, "I have done this and that myself, and know it can

be done, and done well, in a certain time."[40] In this view, self-reliance is promoted more for the sake of buttressing the authority and confidence of employers than for the sake of abolishing a role that strains the expectations of democratic equality.

Rotating or sharing the work stood as a powerful alternative to abolishing the servant's role through self-help or a technological fix. In an attempt to perform their own work collectively, forty households in Cambridge, Massachusetts, banded together in 1869 in a cooperative housekeeping arrangement. This effort to eliminate servants lasted only a year, however, and failed, according to one participant, because most of the women faltered in the face of the hard work necessary for its success.[41] Recognizing that self-sufficiency is difficult, many placed their hope in a servantless home supported from the outside by an array of commercial services. Akin to Bellamy's vision, commercial laundries would accomplish the washing and ironing, and kitchens the cooking. By moving housework to the public and professional spheres, the segmentation of work and home would be nearly complete and the home would become a more pure haven of rest, leisure, and mutual affection.[42] But no commercial establishments could tend to daily needs as immediately as servants, and the commercialization of housework did not create a servantless middle-class home. At least for the nineteenth century, domestic service and its problems would persist.

Contractual Boundaries

The servant's role persisted because employers continued to demand *personal* service. The most effective reform was aimed directly at this demand, by imposing contractual boundaries on the job. Harriet Beecher Stowe, Catharine Beecher, and later Lucy Maynard Salmon all insisted on a fundamental yet practical reform: founding the servant role more solidly on a contractual basis, and thereby limiting employers' demands. The point of the contract was not to ensure that servants consented nominally to their jobs; rather it was to restructure the job by placing firm boundaries around it. Lingering feudal assumptions about the servant's place, the Beechers noted, supported among employers a "spirit of superiority" and a "latent spirit of something like contempt" for servants. The respect and courtesy that servants deserved as moral equals could come only when the relation between servant and employer was "precisely that of a person who for money provides any kind of service for you." They asserted that servants should be allowed to leave and enter the house as they wished without any meddling in their personal business. The authority of the master and mistress of the house should extend only to those specific jobs servants had contracted to perform. In addition, servants should be provided with comfortable rooms and time for relaxation, and be treated as people "having the same human wants" as their employers. Only when hiring servants was approached as a business matter defined by "cool contract" rather than blindly guided by feudal habit would the burdens of the servant problem be lightened.[43]

Forty-five years later, Lucy Maynard Salmon elaborated this suggestion and offered several concrete ways of strengthening the contractual relation between employer and servant. Servants, she said, should participate in the economic aspects of keeping a household. If damages they caused to household items were deducted from their pay, so they should be given a share of any savings their efforts realized. Sharing in the economic benefits and burdens of a household would replace the aristocratic union of masters and servants. Combined with the sort of thorough respect that would increase the social status of servants, and other developments such as a more scientific approach to household education, these efforts would, Salmon hoped, ameliorate the servant problem.[44]

Contractual relations would, these reformers hoped, establish a clear demarcation between work time and a servant's own time, between the arena of the master's and mistress's authority and the servant's independence. If the work itself could never give servants something to live for, the contract would protect the space for leisure within which servants might find something worthy of living for. Lucy Salmon, for instance, hoped that a clear contractual footing, together with commercial alternatives to housework, would transform domestic service into a part-time job that allowed servants to live in their own homes. This would transform the work by limiting the scope of an employer's authority and securing an independent sphere for servants. The contract, it was hoped, would protect the space within which servants could pursue their own ends. The limitations and boundaries that contracts impose—rather than the moral quality of the consent they involve—made them the most practical model for restructuring work to fit the basic claims of democratic citizens.

None of these proposed reforms was successful in abolishing or even in greatly alleviating the servant problem in the nineteenth century, although the general approaches—abolishing, sharing, and restructuring work—remain the fundamental ways of addressing work that constitutes a bad fit.[45] The servant problem abated because of technology: washing machines and electric ovens, refrigerators and vacuum cleaners—these realized the dream of a servant-less home. Elementary as these devices have become, one can scarcely appreciate the social progress they have afforded. Domestic service was once among the most numerically important occupations in the land; today it is a very minor job category.[46] To appreciate the progress technological development has enabled, one must understand the dimensions of the problem that once faced Americans.

Technology has relaxed but not eliminated the problem with service work. With the decline of servant labor, middle-class Americans (principally women) again became responsible for household chores, and the contemporary rise of two-career couples has made the undertaking of these tasks again a thorny matter.[47] Nor is it likely that machines will ever carry out many of the most important responsibilities that remain fixed in the household. Although televisions may "help," no machine can raise children. The "time bind" that constrains working couples has made nannies and childcare workers common in affluent homes. Often these caregivers come from abroad, driven by poverty to leave their own children in order to care for those of others, and here the problem of fit resurfaces.[48] This problem often does not derive from a failure to secure consent or contracts of mutual advantage; it is rather a matter of protecting the elemental space in which workers pursue their own purposes and ends. Attending to the claims of fit is an urgent matter for those who take democratic equality seriously and affirm that no one is born to serve others. Democratic citizens take themselves to be free. Yet as Will Kymlicka argues, "Freedom of choice is not valued for its own sake, but as a precondition for pursuing those projects and practices that *are* valued for their own sake."[49] Work worthy of choice requires the kinds of work roles that are fitting for free, equal, and proud democratic citizens.

5

The Work Ethic and Callings

When work leaves no space for the expression of pride that attends those who take themselves to be moral equals—when it displaces the room to live a life of one's own—work fails to fit the basic expectations of democratic citizens. The sense of dignity that democracy affirms supports some minimal understanding of fit, where work is bounded so as to enable citizens to pursue ends of their own. But as we have seen, liberal democracy also needs to affirm the value of work, especially in contrast to the aristocratic ideal of leisure. Democracy assumes citizens are capable of self-government and self-direction, without the stewarding care of rulers who stand as eternal parents. Democratic citizens need to take responsibility for their own material support.[1] The work ethic expresses a kind of reciprocity, since work is one of the most potent ways in which we express the "duty to contribute to the prosperity of the republic."[2] A generalized work ethic also establishes an equality of condition (everyone works), which is not so extensive as to give all the same material wealth or social status but still imposes a rough similarity in the way of life democratic citizens pursue. As Tocqueville recognized, the removal of social and legal barriers to ambition unleashes pride, as each can hope to distinguish himself from others. Yet the distinguished generate envy. "One must never blind oneself," Tocqueville writes, "to the fact that democratic institutions most successfully develop sentiments of envy in the human heart."[3] Against this tendency stands not only the view that "all work is honorable" but also the notion that all have a duty to work.

This affirmation comes into focus in the work ethic. In part, this is an ethic of responsibility and diligence. It asks that we avoid becoming a burden to others by taking basic responsibility for ourselves. Yet the claim for the work ethic also involves something deeper. The classic account of the work ethic involves a profound understanding of how work might fit us, central to which is the concept of the calling. The calling makes sense of the diligence that work enjoins by describing not only why it is good for the regime that we work responsibly, but also why it is good for us. More than a basic or minimal fit, callings involve an ideal fit in which our most central and definitive purposes are aligned with our work.

Worries about the Work Ethic

Some ethic of work has retained its grip: as we saw in Chapter 2, Americans appear to be working as hard as ever.[4] Amid the hard reality of declining real wages and the difficulty of balancing work with family, no one suggests that the disposition to work reflects manufactured needs or false promises. Nor does all this work breed resentment. Job satisfaction levels are consistently high, in spite of economic vagaries and declining faith in social institutions: for the past forty years, a steady 80 percent of workers have reported being satisfied with their jobs.[5] Young people—their "slacker" image notwithstanding—endorse hard work much like their elders.[6] At least in terms of the hours people work and their satisfaction on the job, there is no crisis in the American work ethic—as we saw in Chapter 2, the affirmation of work is as urgent as ever.

Still, the worry persists that the work ethic in America is insufficient or unreliable and needs the auxiliary support of more forceful exhortation and stronger economic incentive.[7] Few are inclined to say that the work ethic in America is "excellent," and many believe that the work ethic is worse now than in the past.[8] This disparity has led some to suggest that an ethic of work is fragile among a minority—especially those who rely in the long run on welfare rather than work for their economic support. Lawrence Mead argues, for instance, that there is a growing gap between most Americans, who are more involved with work and are working longer hours, and the nonworking poor, who resist the discipline of work.[9] Anxieties seem to nag at the formidable ethic of work Americans exhibit, as if that ethic is more fragile than it appears.

Perhaps working hours and job satisfaction statistics are not the best measure of the work ethic. The work ethic not only asks something of individuals—that they work conscientiously and diligently—but also something of work. Mead, for instance, also speculates that the work ethic is in decline for Americans in general, not because they are less likely to be diligent but because they are less able to find meaning in their work. Many, he notes, "find little connection between their personal efforts and their own rewards."[10] Diligence is not the same as the work ethic. Moreover, the values of both the left and the right can serve as reproaches to the common life of work, which often neither reflects individuals' autonomous choices nor generates great wealth. So even while people work as hard as they did in the past, the perception of an imperiled work ethic may hold true. If the internal meaning of the work has shifted, if a newer and more fragile ethic or habit of work has replaced the old work ethic, then the sense that the work ethic is in decline is consistent with the fact that most people still work hard.

The ethic or habit of work stands in contrast to broader notions of the work ethic that situate ordinary work within a religious conception of living well. The persistent concern about the work ethic stems from the gap between our diligence and our ability to attribute meaning and purpose to the working life. As the work ethic has been transformed into a habit of diligence, the old understandings that supported the deeper ethic have lost their hold. Adequate incentives support a will to work, but they lack the moral underpinnings provided by the older work ethic. In its Protestant version, this ethic grounded dutiful diligence in the doctrine of the calling. The calling explained why individuals could fit their work in a profound and complete way. It supplied diligence with a deeper meaning and broader purpose than economic incentive alone can offer. Absent these, the contemporary habit of work lingers, though as something spare and vulnerable, the object of concern and doubt.

An Ethic Transformed

A number of prominent social critics of the past century illuminated the transformation of the work ethic into a more hollow ethic of work. Once "one of the most important underpinnings of American culture," Christopher Lasch writes, the work ethic has been replaced with an ethic of survival.[11] In its original meaning, the work ethic was not about gain but self-denial. "The self-made man," Lasch notes, "archetypical embodiment of the American dream, owed his advancement to habits of industry, sobriety, moderation, self-discipline, and avoidance of debt."[12] These virtues may have brought wealth, but they were valued independently of it. The work ethic brought achievement, but this was measured less against other people and more against the natural world and the destructive temptations of one's own nature. But in a shift that began at the turn of the twentieth century, on Lasch's account, the virtues of self-mastery gave way to the demands of image manipulation and ordinary desire. The growth of large corporate organizations and the advent of consumer credit weakened the claims of self-restraint and altered the object of competition from triumph over self to victory over others.

The challenges of sustained effort and mastery of craft receded, and in their place came the need to appear personable and confident: "Today men seek the kind of approval that applauds not their actions, but their personal attributes," Lasch says. Where people once dominated by Protestant virtues of thrift, focus, and sobriety might succumb to pride, the new types are simply vain—more proud of how they appear and what they have than what they are and have accomplished. Animated by the new ethic, people seek celebrity rather than recognition for lasting achievement, according to Lasch. Celebrity is preferred to admiration because it does not demonstrate any triumph over adversity and because it carries more power to gratify one's desires. And gratification, in the current age, is what ultimately motivates work, in Lasch's view. A hedonistic ethic motivates and legitimates work, depriving work of its inner meaning and making it always a means to some pleasure found outside it. Even socializing and friendship, which used to provide some respite from the demands of labor, are reduced to a kind of networking that facilitates getting ahead. Where the work ethic asked for fortitude, the new ethic of work demands the emotional intelligence necessary to manipulate others. "The growth of bureaucracy, the cult of consumption with its immediate gratifications, but above all the severance of the sense of historical continuity," Lasch summarizes, "have transformed the Protestant ethic while carrying the underlying principles of capitalist society to their logical conclusion. The pursuit of self-interest, formerly identified with the rational pursuit of gain and the accumulation of wealth, has become a search for pleasure and psychic survival."[13]

On Lasch's reading of modern America, the most obvious sign of the work ethic—hard work—persists while the work ethic itself recedes, replaced by what was once its opposite, the determination to win new pleasures. The claims of marketing, which play to the very weakness against which the work ethic was meant to defend, eroded the old ethic. Like Lasch, Daniel Bell too noted the erosion of the old work ethic in the face of these challenges, and he too located the shift in the early years of the twentieth century, when the allure of buying on credit displaced the negative connotations of debt, and when consumption—facilitated by credit rather than independent achievement—became the end of work. Left in the eclipse of the Protestant ethic, Bell contends, is the dark world of petty hedonism, which becomes the justification of capitalist enterprise. But work for the sake of consumption leaves capitalism with no "transcendent ethic." Where better comforts and the "glorification of plenty" justify capitalism, work and accumulation are stripped of internal meaning, and cannot stand as ends that transcend the sundry desires that themselves often fail to produce lasting satisfaction.[14]

Undermined by the very capitalism it once promoted, the old work ethic—an ethic that heralded work's internal dignity and importance and linked work with self-discipline and even self-denial for the sake of contribution and individual achievement—no longer underwrites the meaning of work. Lacking that "transcendental" justification, work is justified by the pleasures it affords and never carries us beyond our terrestrial predicament. Work stands always as our necessity, or rather as inescapably necessary for the satisfaction of earthly desires, but it cannot connect the satisfaction of desire with anything more lasting. If Lasch and Bell are right, then Americans work as hard as before but with less reason, or for a lower reason, than we might if we were still animated by the old work ethic.

To assess this claim we must look beyond the nineteenth-century work ethic Lasch and Bell had in view to the Protestant ethic that preceded it. For there one can see more clearly how the fortitude and self-denial that Lasch and Bell pointed to were linked to the individual's own purposes. These qualities were not, in the Protestant ethic, simply sacrificial. They did not, for instance, require simply that we overcome our own desires for the sake of serving society. They were connected with salvation, the most important purpose an individual could know. The work ethic in its Protestant form offered a way of understanding why we optimally fit our work, however ordinary. This description of the work ethic was most powerfully advanced by Max Weber, whose claim for the link between Protestant asceticism and an ethic of work helpful to capitalist development remains one of the most insightful and provocative arguments in modern social science.

The Protestant Ethic: Max Weber

Nothing could be farther from the Protestant ethic Weber described than the hedonist justification of work that Lasch and Bell identify in the contemporary setting. In Weber's account, the Protestant injunction to work, and the ethic of work, are not for the sake of attaining better comforts nor for any future worldly enjoyment. On the contrary, Weber insists, the Protestant work ethic was not derived from any interest in the "joy of living" nor even from the importance of "satisfying material needs." For the Protestant ethic, which legitimated and even entailed accumulation, also carried a corollary injunction "to avoid all spontaneous enjoyment of life."[15] The Protestant ethic of Weber's description is distinct from the contemporary work ethic in that it does not justify work in terms of the earthly satisfactions work might place within reach.

Hard work for the sake of comfort and even opulence is nothing new—one need not be a hedonist to work for the sake of satisfying desire. The radicalness of the Protestant ethic is found in the way it freed the injunction to hard work from familiar reasons rooted in rapacious acquisitiveness and unrestrained greed. At the same time, it established a duty to work that stood independent of the traditional aim of satisfying customary expectations. The ethic tempered ambition and desire by decoupling accumulation and earthly power: accumulation through work was for its own sake. By making work an end in its own right, it also infused ambition into traditional complacency: "A man does not 'by nature' wish to earn more and more money," Weber says, "but simply to live as he is accustomed to live and to earn enough for that purpose."[16] Work as its own end breaks the link between needs or desires and the effort required to satisfy them, and so bestirs the traditionally minded to work more and with greater intensity, while it demands that those of great ambition and desire work for something outside themselves. But what does it mean for work to be its own end? Only by understanding how in the Protestant ethic work is an end in itself can we begin to see why the Protestant work ethic involved a worldly asceticism, and glimpse the consequences of the loss of such an ethic for the justice of work.

Without a notion of work as its own end, the Protestant work ethic appears utterly irrational, Weber notices, for the ethic divorces the motive to work from the fruits of one's labors. It reverses the natural relation between work and the rest of life. Naturally, work is for the sake of life, Weber assumes. Since work is instrumental, from the perspective of this natural relation, living for the sake of work is irrational. Ask an individual "filled with the spirit of capitalism," Weber suggests, what is the point of his "restless activity," and although at some loss to answer, he will perhaps say that he hopes to provide for his family. But probe more deeply, and one will find that for these sorts of people, "business with its continuous work has become a necessary part of their lives." Continuous work is necessary, but not instrumentally so. This necessity "expresses what is, from the view-point of personal happiness, so irrational about this sort of life, where a man exists for the sake of his business, instead of the reverse." The spirit of capitalism is ascetic, as accumulation is not for the sake of opulence and luxury. He who ideally expresses the spirit of capitalism "gets nothing out of his wealth for himself, except the irrational sense of having done his job well," Weber says.[17]

Such is the strange and radical way that the Protestant ethic transforms work. It enables a devotion to work and accumulation that previously, and perhaps still, seems contrary to nature and reason. Without the Protestant ethic, work is necessary for the sake of life, or beyond that, for a life of comfort, status, and power. But the Protestant ethic makes work a kind of moral duty rather than a material or instrumental necessity. The internalization of this duty gives rise to a new kind of necessity emanating from a habit or ethic that replaces the natural necessity rooted in survival. Is this dutiful approach to work rational, or, as Weber's comments suggest, does the Protestant ethic of work ultimately lack reason?

The Spur of Devotion

Weber suggests that the Protestant ethic flows from anxiety rather than reason. What mattered to the Calvinist was not earthly achievement but salvation. Yet salvation was reserved for the chosen, and the doctrine of predestination meant that none could be certain of being among the chosen. No free decision, no cultivation of virtues, no laudable actions could affect one's eternal destiny. The generation that accepted this doctrine, Weber speculates, must have known "a feeling of unprecedented inner loneliness of the single individual." Beyond any earthly assistance, each was "forced to follow his path alone to meet a destiny which was decreed for him from eternity." Amid such spiritual isolation, no one could avoid wondering and doubting whether he was included among the elect. The inevitable uncertainty produced, Weber says, a determination to muster—or to feign when one could not muster—complete conviction in oneself as one of the elect, "since lack of self confidence is the result of imperfect faith, hence of imperfect grace." The best way to generate that confidence was through dedication to work. This "alone disperses religious doubts and gives the certainty of grace," by providing visible evidence, through good works, of one's state of grace.[18]

On this view, an anxious uncertainty about one's salvation motivates an impulse to manifest through work the outward signs of salvation. If work is not for the sake of its immediate rewards, it is not exactly for its own sake either. Rather, it aims to support the conviction of one's salvation. Although work itself, no matter how successful, never directly brings about salvation, it may sustain a sense of the salvation that can never be earned or achieved through effort. But even generating this sense or conviction is an achievement, and it demands persistent devotion to labor. For work to produce the signs of grace, both outward and psychological, it must not be occasional but consistent. The manifestation of grace is not infrequent good works that balance out intermittent sins, but the creation of a life that over its whole demonstrates its blessed character. The object of work is to show oneself as an instrument of God's overall plan, which is why the Protestant ethic demands devotion to work over a whole life. Work needs to be sustained, systematic, and methodical if it is to increase God's earthly glory to the greatest extent—and so also be a convincing signal that the worker is one of God's elect. "The God of Calvinism," Weber writes, "demanded of his believers not single good works, but a life of good works combined into a single system."[19] The deep spiritual loneliness and anxiety about one's state of grace is, on this account, the original spring of the work ethic.

The Protestant ethic lifts work out of its natural location as it makes the necessity of work independent of the material needs for which it provides. Precisely speaking, the Protestant ethic does not make work its own end but treats work as if it were a means of connecting ordinary work with divine works by inducing people to show through their daily work that they are among God's chosen. Thus the Protestant ethic sanctifies ordinary productive endeavor, giving work a reason that transcends our earthly predicament by connecting with the divine what would otherwise be a profane response to material need and human desires. Work without limit, irrational from the perspective of individual happiness, becomes rational when viewed from the perspective of demonstrating one's faith and divine grace.

It is crucial to see that although the Protestant ethic renders systematic accumulation rational, the sanctification of work does not extend to the worldly comfort and opulence that accumulation enables. The Protestant ethic enjoins work without limit but does not officially loosen restraints on spending or enjoyment. The prosperous as well as the poor must adhere to the discipline of frugality. The Protestant ethic makes work, like contemplation or prayer, one of the activities through which people transcend their natural inclinations and approach the divine. Asceticism is no longer relegated to a monastic life; asceticism becomes worldly as work becomes linked with the otherworldly.

Diligence in a Calling

One can see immediately how far the contemporary "work ethic" is from its ancestor: though it demands dedication to work, the contemporary ethic neglects to privilege earning or accumulation over spending and enjoyment. Lasch and Bell seem quite right to note that it appears founded on something much more like hedonism than the ascetic denial Weber describes as integral to the Protestant ethic. Many now work for the rewards they find in this life rather than for confidence in their everlasting salvation, and the chase after earthly rewards produces its own terrestrial anxiety. Yet besides the interest in proving salvation, the older work ethic contained another element that provides an even stronger reason for work than salvation anxiety: the doctrine of the calling.

As a product of concern about salvation, the ethic of work seems without reason in the strict sense, since the effort of work could in no case actually produce salvation or enhance its prospect. That diligence could mollify anxiety about salvation gave the work ethic a psychological reason, and made the habit of hard work understandable. But the doctrine of the calling offered a deeper reason for diligent work. Familiar enough prior to the Reformation, callings were limited to those who were called to the exclusive service of God. Monks and clerics followed their callings away from the ordinary activities of the world, and thus removed from common temptations and travails, they could attain a higher state of grace. The Reformation generalized callings to cover all honest occupations, and in elevating ordinary labor also denied monastics their exclusive vocational status. Because the monastery turned away from society and separated its inhabitants from those carrying out God's earthly business, it could not be the location of a legitimate calling.[20]

The extension of the calling or vocation to include all ordinary

occupations is at the core of the Protestant ethic of work because it
links every sort of honest labor with divine purpose. Approaching
work as a calling makes labor a duty instead of a curse. The calling
establishes work's necessity apart from our material necessity. But
taking work to be a calling also requires that individuals see themselves related to their jobs in a way that is not accidental or arbitrary. Callings, in short, involve a fit between individuals and their
work that not only links individual aptitudes with specific occupations but also connects work, however ordinary, with the highest
purposes individuals can serve. The religious context of the calling
justifies work by establishing a fit between work and our highest
purposes. By connecting work to an individual's most urgent ends,
callings establish not merely a basic fit but an ideal one between individuals and their work. As such they underwrite a commitment
and devotion to the working life.

The Democratic Order

By generalizing the calling to cover all occupations, the Calvinist
ethic wrought a radical change on the older web of Thomistic understandings of place and hierarchy. The older view differentiated
between religious vocations approaching the sacred and the range
of profane occupations in which people find themselves by chance,
but in which they also have a duty to remain. On the traditional
view, Weber says, obedience to God's will meant accepting the limits of one's place. In one respect, Weber is right. Consider, for instance, William Perkins's seventeenth-century account of callings.
Perkins held that every member of the church possessed a "personal
calling" orienting him toward a specific occupation. One source of
personal callings, according to Perkins, is the distinction "by order, whereby God hath appointed, that in every society one person
should be above or under another; not making all equal."[21]

But the leveling force of the calling overpowers whatever justification of hierarchy it might provide. For although God appoints
distinctions by order, God also bestows the "inward gifts" that ori-

ent individuals toward particular callings; as everyone is presumed to possess some gift, so everyone has a calling, and the duty to work diligently in a calling applies without exception. "Every person of every degree, state, sex, or condition without exception must have some personal and particular calling to walk in," Perkins insists. As each must have a calling, so each calling must contribute to the common good—the gifts God bestows on individuals have a social purpose. The "final cause or end of every calling," Perkins proclaims, is "for the benefit and good estate of mankind."[22] To pursue one's calling in a contrary way for private benefit is an abuse of calling or, more precisely, an abuse of the gifts that make one fit for a given calling. The failure to make a social contribution through regular work is, for example, why the "monkish kind of living is damnable," he says. In their isolation, monks are of little use to the larger society. Similarly, since they also live off of society rather than for society, both aristocratic gentlemen and beggars are in a damnable state, according to Perkins. Other occupations fall short on the measure of social contribution too, such as waiting servants, who spend so much time idle and exercise so few skills that they become "fit for no calling."

From the duty to serve society no one is exempt: every one, Perkins says, "rich or poor, man or woman, is bound to have a personal calling, in which they must perform some duties for the common good, according to the measure of the gifts that God has bestowed upon them." Callings demand without exception the methodical application of one's individual aptitudes toward the common benefit. This universal command to labor in a calling introduces a new source of social order that works not so much by directly justifying hierarchy as by exacting methodical and sustained effort. Just as each must have a calling, so must each exert himself diligently and painfully in that calling. Work in a calling cannot be irregular or subject to the vagaries of material want and need; callings demand regular effort focused on a specific job. This devotion to a specific task helps avoid the "confusion and disorder" that arises when individuals envy others their places. Fixed on a particular calling, each may turn his ambition to serving God through serving others.[23] Overturning the order that placed aristocrats and clerics above laborers and peasants, the radical extension of callings provided the basis for a new order by issuing the certain conviction that every person in fact has an inner call to pursue a "settled course," with sustained devotion.[24] Notwithstanding secular distinctions in rank and authority, the democratic extension of callings gave equal honor to every place of industry; it dignified every sort of honest and useful occupation. But as the extension of calling sanctified ordinary life, so it also deprived the world of a sacred sphere insulated from ordinary life and higher than the sphere of work.

The calling thus powerfully unifies the several strands of justification that bear on the justice of work. The calling manages to reconcile the social fit of Plato's *Republic* with personal fit. It does this by connecting our aptitudes as they are revealed in the market with our most important purpose, salvation. The calling asks believers to understand their aptitudes not as arbitrary natural endowments but instead as intentional and sacred gifts. The calling establishes the justice of ordinary work by linking it not to transient pleasures but to more urgent ends that stand higher than earthly rewards.

Wealth and the Work Trap

The kind of fitting work that the Protestant ethic offered was subject to an inner strain that makes the ethic unstable, at least in its strong Calvinist form. Although the work ethic demands worldly asceticism, it also legitimates and encourages accumulation—and wealth, as the Puritan divines knew well, can exert an irresistible pressure on ascetic habits. Complying with the demands of asceticism is always trying, and far more so when one possesses the degree of wealth that enables satisfaction and indulgence. This is the central difficulty in the original Protestant ethic: turning people toward labor in this world without turning their focus solely to the rewards of this world, which become increasingly attainable through the methodical and diligent labor that the ethic enjoins. Shorn of its connection to God's purposes and individual salvation, the work ethic loses its deepest purposive dimension. Without the connection to divine purpose, work becomes strictly a worldly affair with purposes wholly secular. The turn to secular purposes privileges money, and in this way, the Protestant ethic becomes an ethic not of work but of wealth.[25]

The transformation from an ethic of work to an ethic of wealth is abetted by the tendency to define aptitudes by reference to market valuation. From the perspective of the Protestant ethic, one's skills and talents are viewed as gifts related not only to social needs but also to divine intention. One locates a calling by taking stock of one's inner gifts. Yet at the same time the end of a calling is to serve the common good. Therefore one's inner gifts must be identified and evaluated in terms of social needs. The tendency to define what is useful in terms of what is profitable makes profit the measure of aptitude and calling. Indeed, profit signals that one occupies an appropriate calling. As one Puritan divine counseled, "If God shows you the way in which you may lawfully get more than another way (without wrong to your soul or any other), if you refuse this, and choose the less gainful way, you cross one of the ends of your calling, and you refuse to be God's steward."[26]

By subordinating aptitudes to usefulness, and defining usefulness in terms of profit, the calling is reduced to the single measure of money making (even if it is not for the sake of spending). Yet profit is a crude and sometimes false sign of social contribution. This the Puritans recognized in the case of usury; we are more apt to identify the disjunction between the common good and market demand in the case of drugs, prostitution, and other socially deleterious though profitable activities. Identifying one's inner gifts and even rendering them of use to others is not the same as maximizing one's take in the market.[27] But how to identify aptitudes or define what is useful, except by the market? Without any convincing answer, the

Protestant ethic was subject on its own terms to a transformation into an ethic of wealth.

A second problem with the Protestant ethic involves the way it relates purposes to work. The Protestant ethic invests great purpose in ordinary work, but in an important way the purpose always remains truncated from the work. The greatness of purpose—serving God and participating in realizing God's intention—is not discovered or amplified through the work itself. Sweeping floors or collecting taxes says little about God's purpose. Faith enjoins one to work diligently in a "settled path," yet it is not the activity of work itself that informs a deeper or more abiding faith. Faith exists first, and the purposes that derive from faith also come prior to work. Only once faith is accepted is everyday work endowed with extraordinary purpose.

By equipping individuals to read back from divine intention, the Protestant ethic invests work with serious purpose and great promise, yet neither the purpose nor the promise emanates from the activity of work. Cleaning house or bricklaying can be seen as an expression of duty only if faith is solid. Work does not mediate between faith, or an apprehension of one's highest purpose, and the demands of everyday life. The Protestant ethic thus suffers from being too reliant on steady will alone to produce and sustain the faith that invests work with its greatest purpose. When the will falters, there is nothing in one's work itself that reconnects it to faith. This is perhaps no problem for steady believers, but it does place an enormous burden on faith. In addition, it allows the Protestant ethic to be used as an ideological tool for eliciting diligence and commitment to work that on its own merits would not generate either. More than the march of modern secularism, this is what lends fragility to the Protestant ethic of work: for when faith wavers, and there is nothing in one's work itself that connects work with faith or broader human purposes, the instrumental purposes of work— wealth and security—stand ready to supplant the overriding purpose given by faith. While the Protestant ethic imposes great purpose on work, it fails to show how work mediates quotidian concerns and faith.

The shift from work to wealth has several important consequences. For one, wealth gained without work stands on a par with wealth accumulated through working—or perhaps stands better, for it avoids the painful self-denial involved in work. Where wealth is the justification of work, the obligation to work diminishes for the rich, since necessity cannot justify their devotion to work. By making material necessity and want the reason to work, the ethic of wealth takes away dignity and honor from work that is not the result of necessity. Work done not out of need comes to look like the foolish result of unthinking, unwarranted, and unshakable habit.

The problem, on Weber's analysis, is that the religious grounding of the calling has withered, yet we remain, like it or not, devoted to work. To Weber's eye, modern workers in general, and workaholic Americans in particular, cannot escape working *as if* it were a calling. We work, and have to work, with devotion, in settled paths, over long hours and sustained years, as if work were its own purpose apart from the money and status that it might bring. We possess a work ethic, yet lack a larger ethic that lends meaning and purpose to our work, because the convictions carried to the world of work by early Protestants have waned. The result, Weber says, is that the ideal of dutiful work in a calling "prowls about in our lives like the ghost of dead religious beliefs."[28] Shorn of the religious convictions that originally supported it, the work ethic rests instead on a combination of blind habit, a steely will to survive amid heartless competition, and the promise of status and physical comfort. While these spurs to work are reliable enough in practice, they support a hollowed-out ethic. Where the ethic in its original form connected work with an individual's highest purpose, without faith the aptitudes we engage in our work retain their economic function but lose their moral dimension.

The allure of consumption has a central place in sustaining the work ethic, and real pleasures attend those material possessions that constitute the American Dream. Nor should the force of blind habit be underestimated. We have inherited a sense of duty about work even though that duty has been divorced from the larger web of meanings that made sense of it. And the work ethic has long been exploited, not least by those who stand to gain by the efforts of those who are willing to work hard and well without a view to their wage. The notion that work is a duty serves as a very useful tool. Yet even more important is the coercive effect of economic competition. When enough others work as if from an ethic, one has to do the same simply to survive, to keep one's job or to stay in business. A casual approach to work is punished by the shared pursuit of profit and productivity, and competition in the market means that disciplined and methodical work generates its own enforcement. For his part, Weber saw the persistence of the work ethic as a trap. Where "the Puritan wanted to work in a calling," Weber famously concludes, "we are forced to do so." Like a "tremendous cosmos," the modern capitalist economy determines the lives of those born into it with "irresistible force." With such force comes the concern for material goods. Although once something that, like a "light cloak," could be thrown off, "fate decreed," Weber says, "that the cloak should become an iron cage."[29] Modern men and women, in this view, have no choice but to give up any aspiration to many-sided development in favor of specialization, to replace a casual approach to life with work beyond reason.

This is exactly the state of affairs that later observers like Christopher Lasch and Daniel Bell described. They sought to recover the sort of purposeful commitment to work that can be justified only if in some important respect work gives us our due. By showing work to be something greater than a response to necessity, the original Protestant ethic gave work dignity. The need to survive and the desire for pleasure are reliable enough incentives to labor—these do not in themselves undercut the inclination to work. But predicating work on these needs and wants places it at the service of lower ends than did the Protestant ethic, and so removes something of work's independent meaning, rendering it less of a duty and making it less clear how we might get our due and serve our best purposes through working. The work ethic asks us to regard our jobs as callings, but the understanding of calling has dropped out of the contemporary understanding of work, which now rests more on the allure of affluence than on any broader faith. Without the understanding of calling, the work ethic stands fragile at its core, lacking an account of work's justice or the full support of reason; it becomes a necessity that would be better avoided were it possible.

Yet perhaps Weber got the fate of the work ethic wrong and it is not so sorry as this suggests. After all, the aspiration to find work that feels like a calling, or work that fits us in some ideal sense, remains a powerful source of both hope and disappointment. It is less a menacing ghost than an enduring point of orientation. Sometimes this hope continues to be expressed in the language of callings, though today the term describes the passion some find in their work more than it does the faith that one is performing a divinely appointed task.[30] The aspiration to find fitting work that is akin to a calling today informs the promise of a fulfilling career. Careers involve competition; in them one aims to ascend over others, and indeed the word *career* originates in the French term for racecourse.[31] But careers pursued for personal fulfillment involve something more than a race. That idea that careers might bring fulfillment suggests that they involve more than interpersonal achievement, that they also contain some intrinsic purpose that makes the work worthy of devotion. But how might careers bring fulfillment? The next chapter turns to John Stuart Mill, who placed great stock in the promise of fulfillment; yet as we will see, Mill thought fulfillment a difficult achievement, and thus resisted generalizing its promise across the world of work.

6

The Promise of Fulfillment

A s the Protestant work ethic devolved to a secular ethic of work, the transcendental purposes served by callings came to be cast as a promise of personal fulfillment. Where the Protestant ethic would have us discern the task to which God appointed us, now we seek to discover the career in which we can find personal fulfillment. The romantic ideal that each person has something unique and valuable to express has been grafted onto an activity—work—that would otherwise be motivated by survival and comfort. Akin to the Protestant ethic, the promise of fulfillment elevates work, investing in it a promise that would make it intrinsically worthwhile, a constituent part of an excellent and happy life. To make sense of the promise of fulfillment and see what is at stake in investing this promise in the working life, we turn to John Stuart Mill, who put individual fulfillment at the center of his liberalism.

Through Mill, we understand how difficult and demanding is the modern ideal of fulfillment. While it constituted the general promise of a liberal society for Mill, later social critics would democratize the promise of fulfillment by mapping it more specifically onto the domain of work—but without calling for the wholesale social transformation that Marx thought a necessary prelude to "freely conscious" or fulfilling work. Yet Mill's own description of fulfillment shows why this effort would likely be disappointed, for Mill conceived of fulfillment in a way that showed it to be something special and rare, demanding uncommon talent and fortitude. Mill's ideal of fulfillment through individuality, or of living a life that is fully our own and not the reflection of values taken secondhand, was an essentially new kind of aristocratic standard. This is not to say that Mill was in any political or social sense an aristocrat: on the contrary, he hoped for and believed in the real possibility of the universal elevation of the moral, intellectual, social, and political powers of human beings. He had no affection or nostalgia for the old order of entrenched inequalities, and held that "all privileged and powerful classes, as such, have used their power in the interest of their own selfishness, and have indulged their self-importance in despising . . . [those] working for their benefit."[1] But at the same time, the ideal of individuality and fulfillment he held up served as a new kind of aristocratic standard in that it was most fully available to only a few: the vigorous, talented, and definitive characters who could achieve it.

Mill's demanding model of fulfillment reflects the way he came to amend and refine, over the early part of his life, the more democratic utilitarianism of Jeremy Bentham, who refused to make qualitative distinctions among pleasures and pains. A qualified democrat and less qualified progressive, Mill came to believe that progress could not be adequately measured by a single scale of pleasure aggregated across an entire population. For Bentham, the human condition could be assessed by an index of pleasure and pain, suitably calibrated to take stock of the various analytical features that are common to all pleasures and pains—for instance, their duration or intensity.[2] Although educated by his father in the spirit of Bentham's humane philosophy, Mill came in the fullness of time—and only through the suffering entailed by a psychic breakdown—to view Bentham's progressivism as radically defective and dispiriting for being overly systematic and rational. A more full and more healthy understanding of ethical and political things, he concluded, would need to more directly address the heart and the spirit.

Poetry would need to complement calculation; Coleridge would be the counterpoise to Bentham: "The cultivation of the feelings became one of the cardinal points in my ethical and philosophical creed," Mill writes.[3] Human well-being would need to be understood more broadly than even Bentham's exacting calculus could measure, and this would be accomplished by including the entire empire of human powers—imaginative, spiritual, sentimental, intellectual, and moral. Rather than reducing the human condition to a single scale of pleasure and pain, it is necessary to embrace, Mill says, "the permanent interests of mankind as a progressive being."[4] Mill understood these interests in terms of individuality, the highest condition we can achieve. Mill's ideal of "individuality" weaves together the romantic value of authenticity, or the revealing of what is definitive, unrepeatable, and ingenious about a specific person, and a more ancient, perfectionist emphasis on development, or the cultivation of the qualitatively higher powers residing in human nature. Both, in a sense, may seem democratic: anyone can be "real," or authentic, as anyone might cultivate his or her higher powers. Yet on examination both turn out to be more discriminating, in that they rely on uncommon capacity and a hierarchical ordering of human capacities. It takes education, practice, and discipline to develop the higher powers of our nature. Authenticity, too, is a formidable achievement that depends on insight and bravery sufficient to overcome the accumulated force of convention. And if human fulfillment as Mill understood it is so difficult, can it be a democratic ideal—can there be an aristocracy of everyone?

The democratization of Mill's ideal would come later, through those of a more popular bent, like Betty Friedan, who invest the common working life with the promise of fulfillment. Yet insofar as these later writers fail to recognize what is difficult and necessarily uncommon about a demanding ideal like fulfillment, they set their readers up for grave disappointments. Fulfillment stands, for Mill, as a difficult and uncommon achievement, one that separates the few from the rest. Not even his identification as a consistent "Radical and Democrat for Europe" can eliminate the aristocratic direction toward which his enlarged conception of human fulfillment tends.[5] Throughout Mill's work, one can feel the strain as his democratic sympathies pull against corresponding aristocratic sympathies. As a radical democrat, Mill cared deeply about the condition of workers; he believed in general that the division between the "capitalist as chief, and workpeople without a voice in management" would be both impossible and undesirable to sustain.[6] In particular, he held that careers open to talents constituted an essential part of a just economy. Mill defended with special vigor the right of women to participate on equal terms in the world of work, in part because he thought it infinitely better for a talented and energetic woman to pursue a career than to "pine through life with the consciousness of thwarted occupations."[7] At the same time he understood stimulating and challenging careers to be the province of the few; more often, work would be a debilitating form of toil, and careers a tiresome field of conformity. At the heart of his feminism was a belief not that careers always offer fulfillment but that marriage should be reformed so that the household would no longer be the site of oppression. He sought to make domestic work worthy of choice.

Individual choice, which is in a sense a lower or more easily satisfied standard than individual fulfillment, is at the core of Mill's understanding of a just society. As a champion of unfettered individual choice, Mill saw the restriction of women to one place—the domicile—as an "anomaly in the modern world" contrary to the "whole stream of modern tendencies." Modernity's "peculiar character," Mill says, is characterized by the conviction that "human beings are no longer born to their place in life" but instead should be free to choose their commitments and roles.[8] Although a defender of choice, Mill did not think all choices equal. He valued choice not only out of respect for the individual freedom to do as one pleases but also because the act of choice crystallized the noblest human faculties. Only in this free and conscious act are "the human faculties of perception, judgment, discriminative feeling, mental activity, and even moral preference, exercised."[9] It is only through an act of choice that human beings can realize their full potential. To grasp how demanding is Mill's ideal of human fulfillment—and thus how difficult it might be to map the promise of fulfillment onto the working life—it is important to identify Mill's hierarchical interpretation of human nature. That Mill found a moral standard in human nature might come as a surprise because of his objection to rooting any ethical standards in nature—an objection that stands, it seems, at the foundation of his feminism and his defense of free choice. Yet as we will see, Mill rejected rooting ethical standards in the physical order of nature only; *human* nature issued in crucial moral standards that ground Mill's ideal of human fulfillment.

Can Nature Be a Standard?

At first Mill might seem to deny that nature can offer any sort of standards for ethical life. In the essay "Nature," Mill contests all doctrines that look to nature as a test of "right and wrong, good and evil, or which in any mode or degree attach merit or approval to following, imitating, or obeying Nature." Beneath the clouds of ambiguity that surround it, the term *nature,* Mill notes, has two fundamental meanings—and neither provides any guide to action. In the first sense, nature refers to all the powers in "the inner or outer world." Understood as all the forces, actual or potential, in the universe, it is nonsensical to take nature as any sort of ethical guide, for everything humans do is natural in this sense. Every human act, Mill says, makes use of some natural power, and all the effects of human action are produced "in exact obedience to some law or laws of nature." Although it is possible to act in ignorance of the laws of nature, often to one's detriment, it is impossible to act contrary to these laws.[10] As human beings are wholly subject to the physical laws of nature, it is impossible that nature in this sense could provide a standard for what we choose to do, or for those institutions we have the power to shape.

If nature is to offer any standard or guidance, it must depend on a separate definition. When nature is used ethically, Mill says, it refers to that which takes place without human intervention. On this view, what human beings bring about by their own power, artifice, and convention might be guided by what comes into being on its own, or what is natural. But to take nature in this sense as an ethical standard would be irrational and immoral. A belief that we should act so as to correspond with what would take place without our intervention would depend on the assumption that nature encompasses a scheme we should not thwart or disobey. Alone, this assumption would enjoin every attempt to amend the course of nature for human benefit: "To dig, to plough, to build, to wear clothes, are direct infringements of the injunction to follow nature," Mill points out. The supposition that we should not interfere with the order of nature would forbid even the most basic efforts at convenience, such as "putting up an umbrella."[11] A belief that what comes into being without human intervention is better than what human beings bring into being through artifice and convention would impugn all civilization, and undermine all efforts made on behalf of improving the human situation.

Mill associates the notion that humans should not meddle in nature's course with the religious suspicion of artifice and the romantic exaltation of instinct over reason. Certain religious views, Mill notes, counsel against amending nature in the name of respecting the plan of an omnipotent and beneficent maker. But nature, understood as what comes into being on its own, often does "things which men are hanged or imprisoned for doing to one another."[12] There is nothing just or right about nature, nor any evidence that nature allocates happiness or suffering in accordance with what people deserve, based on their demonstrated good or evil acts. Nature often kills the noblest of men without the slightest regret, while sparing the wicked. Storms that wipe out crops, or diseases that spread unchecked, kill millions. Even if it were right that these misfortunes and tragedies at the hands of nature are all for the best because all belong to God's plan, this would give human beings no reason to take nature as a guide and to imitate it.

Nor does human nature offer any direct ethical guide. Mill forthrightly rejects the idea that the innate tendencies or instincts of human beings lead to morality or virtue. Left to our innate tendencies, Mill says, few people would develop any virtue; on the contrary, human goodness and perfection require subduing or redirecting nature, and in some cases conquering our nature. Where virtue bids us to be courageous, for instance, instinct would often have us flee in the face of danger. Even the virtue of cleanliness, Mill supposes, would often be overrun by the innate tendency to slovenliness. As for veracity, Mill holds that instinct alone would often have us lie; contrary to Rousseau, Mill asserts, "savages are always liars." More to the point, Mill notes that many instincts are positively contrary to morality, such as the urge to destroy, the desire to dominate, and, darkest of all, the tendency to take pleasure in cruelty. To take nature as an ethical guide, to assume that innate instincts or tendencies are the expression of some beneficent design, would justify "the most atrocious enormities," Mill says, for nothing is more central to the order of nature, or better expresses the natural urge to dominate, than the idea that "the strong should prey on the weak."[13] Morality does not require nature to show it the way; rather, nature needs to be amended and constrained in accordance with morality. Morality should take its standard not from nature, Mill argues, but from utility. Only by considering what conduces to the general good can we know what in nature it is right to encourage, amend, or resist.

The one principle we can read from nature is that the strong prey on the weak: in this respect, the subjection of women is "natural." But physical domination does not supply its own justification; argument must complement force. The argument for restricting the rights and opportunities of women, Mill notes, is the same as that used by slaveholders in the southern United States, and by Aristotle, to justify slavery: women are intended by nature, and therefore are suited by nature, to the domestic role. But since nature cannot provide the basis of morality, Mill argues, this argument cannot justify the subjection of women.[14]

The Subjection of Women

Mill's argument about the ethical irrelevance of nature sits at the foundation of his famous case against the subjection of women. It is also what leads him to advocate an ethic of free choice: because nature does not fit us to certain social roles, each person should be free to choose. A just allocation of work would simply reflect the free choices of individuals, and the conditions of socially necessary work (such as domestic labor) should be reformed so that the work is choiceworthy. Because nature offers no standard for the social division of labor, any restrictions on individual choice—such as those that burdened all women—are unjust.

While he clearly thinks it false, Mill patiently explores the assumption that natural differences between the sexes entail distinct social roles. Obviously nature could not cause women to be wives and mothers and nothing else, or legal force would be superfluous. Nor is it clear, Mill insists, that women have by nature the disposition or incipient talents that uniquely equip them for a domestic role. The true nature of women cannot be seen, he says, because what men see in women and what women see in themselves is not nature but history. We cannot know how many, if any, of the differences between men and women with regard to intellectual ability and temperament are due to nature, without peeling away the effects of custom, prejudice, and education, all of which aim at producing precisely those differences so often attributed to nature. Whether women possess different or lesser capabilities by nature cannot be known because these capacities "have never been called out," Mill says. Aside from the degree to which women's intellectual qualities are attributable to nature, even what women think must be shrouded, for so long as men have power over women, and women have the duty to obey men, women cannot speak with "complete sincerity and openness." Women's characteristics, wrongly attributed to nature, are more likely a matter of artifice, Mill observes. For men want in their women not only a sort of slave but also a willing slave, and given wives' dependence on husbands, "it would be a miracle if the object of being attractive to men had not become the polar star of feminine education and formation of character," Mill explains.[15] Veiled by the social forces of education and expectation, perverted in its expression because of the vast disparity in power, women's nature cannot be discerned with enough accuracy and precision to justify any social arrangements.

The real reason for restricting women to the domestic sphere, as Mill unmasks it, is the social necessity of domestic work. This truth, Mill argues, should be exposed to the light and fully examined: "I should like to hear somebody openly enunciating the doctrine, 'It is necessary to society that women should marry and produce children. They will not do so unless they are compelled. Therefore it is necessary to compel them.'"[16] On this view, there is a profound conflict between the needs of society and the claims of individuals, or between our social fit and our personal fit. But the claim that social fit requires coercion, whether made on behalf of restricting women's roles, impressing sailors, or enforcing slavery, is "open to retort," for it rests on a "Hobson's choice" that refuses to contemplate transforming or altering roles that will not be adequately filled short of coercion. In the case of sailors and slaves, Mill notes, the argument depends on a refusal to pay the fair value of labor. Here Mill suggests that consenting to a wage diminishes, if it does not fully erase, the conflict between individual desert and social need. Perhaps, then, the solution for women's roles is to pay a market wage for the work women provide in the household. But Mill does not suggest that domestic work should be commodified and made like any other job. Rather, he suggests changing the terms of the marriage contract to make marriage a sort of unpaid career that can compete without the benefit of coercion against other paid careers.

Marriage on new terms, based on equality, would depend on ensuring for women the power of earning, along with women's independent right to hold property. Formal economic equality—the right to work and earn—is necessary to factual equality within the household, in Mill's view, and only with equality in the household will women consent to marriage without the necessity of legal sanction or coercion. The terms of marriage Mill advocated aim for a union of equal companions, and this, Mill says, would not only be more attractive to women but, just as important, would elevate men. The conventional marriage, between two persons unequal in education, rights, and legal status, elicits the worst from men, who, Mill contends, "reserve the violent, the sulky, the undisguisedly selfish side of their character for those who have no power to withstand it." At the same time, the narrow scope and petty objects of female education in Mill's day meant that a conventional marriage between unequals lacked "mental communion." Once ambitious and curious, men after marriage acquired "new and selfish interests created by the family," and ended up little different from those who wish only for "the common vanities and common pecuniary objects."[17]

Better, Mill insists, to aim for a marriage "where each of the two persons, instead of being a nothing, is a something; where they are attracted to each other, . . . share in each other's tastes, enrich each other's natures, as two friends." In the marriage that subjugates women, women of pluck and ambition often suffer the profound unhappiness "produced by the feeling of a wasted life." Marriage could be worthy of women's free choice only under new terms of association that aspired to form a marriage of companions, with each educated to the same human ends, and each possessing the power to earn and be self-supporting. And only such a marriage would improve both men and women, thereby serving the "moral regeneration of mankind."[18]

While Mill advocated that men and women be equals in "rights and cultivation," and although he insisted careers be equally open to women's talents, Mill did not suppose that with equal rights husbands and wives would in fact fill similar roles, for instance by sharing equally in paid work, child rearing, and household chores. Nor did he suggest that all housework, often performed off market by housewives, be entirely converted to paid market work. Even in Mill's ideal of a companionate marriage, he assumes that women, in choosing marriage, accept a distinct role that carries the primary responsibility for the home and children. Accepting marriage would be akin to choosing a career and agreeing to perform a certain kind of work. Mill states: "Like a man when he chooses a profession, so, when a woman marries, it may in general be understood that she makes choice of the management of a household, and the bringing up of a family, as the first call upon her exertions, during as many years of her life as may be required for the purpose; and that she renounces, not all other objects and occupations, but all which are not consistent with the requirements of this." But why should wives rather than husbands, accept "primary responsibility" for children and the household, and further, why did Mill—who indicted conventional marriage with all its assumptions about women's nature—endorse the "common arrangement" where men earn and women tend the household as "the most suitable division of labor between the two persons"?[19]

Mill does not explicitly consider the possibility that household tasks and paid work outside the home might be shared, nor that wives and husbands might reverse the common division of labor, although all of his arguments indicate that he would view this neither as unnatural nor intrinsically wrong. Very likely, he would have viewed sharing all roles as unworkable without serious political intervention in the tasks associated with child rearing. Although he thought "*laisser-faire,* in short, should be the general practice," he believed the state should both require and provide an elementary education to the children of the working classes.[20] Whether the state should provide child care was not a question Mill took up, and his analysis of the bounds of state intervention leaves the matter an open question in his terms. On one hand, the value Mill sets on individual liberty suggests that he would have been suspicious that vastly increasing the state's role in child rearing would dampen the development of true individuality and extend the soft but effective tyranny of custom and popular opinion.[21] Mill's celebration of individuality, on the other hand, might have prompted him to welcome the reversal or full sharing of men's and women's traditional roles, and quite obviously Mill believed that women could perform in the traditionally male world of paid careers with perfect competence.

Whether men would—not so much whether they could—take up the slack at home and adequately perform the domestic role remains quite another question. What is clear is that to the extent Mill endorsed the traditional division of labor, his endorsement was secondary to his defense of women's equality. He also plainly rejects the proposition that any sex-based division of labor is ordained or sanctioned by nature. Few have leveled such a sustained and persuasive assault on the view that nature calls on women to fill the roles of homemaker and full-time mother rather than paid laborer or professional. Indeed, Mill's argument about nature extends to all attempts to justify social arrangements by some reference to nature. Mill turns—or appears to turn—away from nature toward social utility for moral justification. Deciding what, in nature, needs to be restrained, amended, encouraged, or fostered, depends on what things "most conduce to the general good," Mill says.[22] All social arrangements must be assessed based on "what an enlightened estimate of tendencies and consequences may show to be most advantageous to humanity in general, without distinction of sex."[23]

The Reappearance of Human Nature

Nature, it seems, cannot be used to justify social arrangements. It can tell us nothing about the social places individuals deserve. In the arguments against the subjection of women, as in his case against founding ethics on observations about nature, we witness the profound force and insight of Mill's democratic liberalism: no fixed places, no constraints on harmless choice, no coercion of some for the sake of others. All this, for Mill as for later liberals, is a matter of justice. Yet in the arguments we have so far canvassed, Mill is not rejecting *any* standard rooted in human nature so much as he is disputing a very particular understanding of nature rooted in Rousseau and adapted for his rhetorical purposes.

As Rousseau conceived it, nature is what precedes language, civilization, and history. But this, some set of primordial instincts and passions, is only one part of our nature. When Mill turns from combating the injustices he perceives to articulating a positive case for the fulfillment a liberal society distinctly makes possible, he grounds his analysis in a very discriminating interpretation of human nature. To take nature only as a set of untutored instincts overlooks those distinctive human aspects of our nature that might direct animalistic desires, and that show human history and civilization to be an expression of *human* nature. This more complete view of human nature as an order of different elements, the lowest of which we share with plants and animals, the higher of which rightly constrain the lower, motivates Mill's understanding of human vices and human virtue.

As Mill points out, virtue is not natural in the sense that it results from blindly following our basic instincts. But this does not render nature morally irrelevant. On the contrary, Mill's discussion of such virtues as courage and truthfulness shows that he believes, much like Aristotle, that virtue often consists in developing habits—through training and under the guidance of reason—that counter the tendency of instinct. Virtue is not simply a convention but reflects an understanding of what human nature makes tempting and what, through decision and reason, it makes possible. Virtue, as Mill discusses it, can be conceived as unnatural only if we read reason out of human nature and render human nature and animal nature the same.

Mill's discussion of vice also reveals the way morality reflects an understanding of human nature. Consider, for instance, his discussion of the worst vice: our desire to dominate. The "delight in exercising despotism, in holding other beings in subjection to our will," Mill argued, was a tendency in human nature most worthy of extermination; yet, he contended, exactly this tendency was nourished by the subjection of women in families. Families based on inequality are, Mill says, a "nursery of vices," a "school of despotism."[24] That those who must bear such despotism suffer gravely is, for most, sufficient reason to detest the desire within human beings to dominate others. Surely the perspective of the victim is enough to motivate liberal resistance to unwarranted domination, for liberals since the Levellers and Locke have asserted that no individual's life exists simply for the petty pleasures of another. Yet when Mill discusses the desire to dominate, he speaks not only of the harm to those who are dominated but also of the corruption of those who dominate. The "moral nature" of men is corrupted when they dominate within the household. Exercising a scope of power at home that is without justification or limit, men fail to develop habits of forbearance and respect, and instead become arrogant, overbearing, and selfish. Giving ourselves over to the pleasures of domination is corrupting because it gratifies the lower parts of the soul at the cost of the higher. Equality at home, in contrast, would spur the "moral regeneration" of men, and that in turn would foster the moral regeneration of society.[25]

The moral regeneration of humanity—progress—depends on constraining base desires for the sake of cultivating the higher, more distinctly human capacities. These higher faculties, which require "mental cultivation," involve "the pleasures of the intellect, of feelings and imagination, and of the moral sentiments" rather than those of "mere sensation." What guides Mill's ordering within human nature that privileges the intellectual capacities? On this, Mill is famously ambiguous. In his case for the distinction between higher and lower pleasures—central to his larger defense of utilitarianism—Mill states that the standard rests with the judgment of those who have tried both higher and lower pleasures. Underlying this claim is the view that one cannot develop and express one's higher intellectual capacities without experiencing and understanding the limits of lower pleasures; thus those who know both sorts of pleasure do not renounce the lower by sheer self-discipline so much as they willingly restrain the lower for the sake of something better; knowing both, and knowing the place of each, they are fully human.[26]

Yet Mill is aware that even among experienced sorts, a "decided preference" about higher and lower pleasures may be absent. In this case, Mill says, the preference of a majority should decide the question. But here Mill avoids describing the actual grounding of the distinction between higher and lower pleasures, for there is little reason to suppose that the preferences of some should decide what are higher pleasures for all, unless some convincingly discern a nonsubjective ordering of capacities within human nature. Indeed, Mill expresses serious doubt that simple preferences can always be an adequate sign of the distinction between higher and lower pleasures: out of "infirmity of character," men often prefer nearer goods to more distant ones, and very commonly, he says, people aim for "everything noble" in their youth, only to, "as they advance in years, sink into indolence and selfishness." Through sorry habituation we can fall away from our highest purposes, for devotion to lower pleasures over time incapacitates us for the higher ones.[27] Most of all, blind conformity to prevailing customs cause some to lose their natural potential, "until by dint of not following their own nature they have no nature to follow: their human capacities are withered and starved."[28]

These tendencies warrant skepticism about everyday preferences, but perhaps not about decided preferences. Preference, for Mill, must be the result of real decision, grounded in judgment and reason. Living according to what is "best and highest in me" requires dedication, striving, and fortitude. This inner strength and resolve to pursue our human perfection Mill sometimes calls "character."[29] So the preference that matters is not simply majority preference but the decided preference of those of character. Character is not common, because nature does not make human perfection easy. Nature simply makes it possible, which reveals that human nature is important morally not for what it makes inevitable or instinctual but for what it makes possible. Human nature provides an array of capacities, "a whole world of possibilities," which require a great deal of discipline for their development and realization.[30] Morality is natural not in the sense that it comes without effort but in the sense that the moral goods of vigorous character and self-development take their cue from the ascertainable structure of human nature, which, while it requires interpretation and cultural support, is not itself a human creation.

The Challenge of Choosing

Mill's understanding of the structure of human nature grounded both his judgments about character and his concept of human perfection. Christian ethics, Mill claimed, which emphasized obedience over nobility, produced "a low, abject, servile type of character," while the force of majority opinion in the democratic age suppresses an important part of practical truth by tending to "raise the low and lower the high." Against the spirit of his age, Mill noted that one advantage of aristocracy was the diversity of views different social stations produced. Looking beyond Christian ethics, Mill admired the ethic of nobility arising from the "purely human" philosophy found in "Greek and Roman sources." Mill's admiration for the qualities of nobility illuminates the nature of his praise for diversity. If Mill valued simple variety as such, he might have defended the separate social roles of men and women for the different viewpoints inculcated by separate roles. But for Mill the diversity worth defending is not simple difference. He cherishes the diversity that, against the dampening force of custom, reveals the exercise of distinctively human faculties striving for perfection.

These faculties come into focus and reveal themselves most fully in the act of choice. Not just any casual choice, but a deliberate choice that "employs all his faculties," is the activity in which man perfects himself. In addition to being deliberate, the choice ultimately reaches past mundane everyday matters to address the largest human concerns about "framing the plan of our life to suit our own character." Unlike "cattle" or "sheep," human beings have the capacity to live by judgment.[31] Mill sought a solution to the mediocrity and conformism typical of liberal democratic regimes dedicated to commerce; he looked for it in self-reliant individuals resistant to customary patterns, insistent on expressing their nature through a life plan they forged independently.

Only from among such independent persons can great thinkers arise, because only they possess the moral courage to venture beyond the partial truth reflected in popular opinion. The most important sort of truth, about how to live, contains an inner tension. Mill says: "Truth, in the great practical concerns of life, is so much a question of reconciling and combining of opposites, that very few have minds sufficiently capacious and impartial to make the adjustment with an approach to correctness, and it has to be made by the rough process of a struggle between combatants fighting under hostile banners."[32]

The apparent conflict within truth makes truth hardly seem whole. If it is a whole, it has many sides, a truth perhaps of many truths. Most individuals see only a single side, or live by one part of this untidy, conflicted truth about the most important practical questions. Yet the courage to live by a part that not many see can make the whole visible to others. Many brave individuals are needed, each living by some part, if anyone is to grasp the whole. The whole truth is not evident to all individuals because our individual nature does not always include the whole of human nature. Like a "tree," human nature "requires to grow and develop on all sides, according to the tendency of inward forces which make it a living thing."[33] But the inward force of any given individual may spur the growth of only one branch. Grasping the whole must be beyond the reach of most, for while we (as common bearers of human nature) share in the possession of great and various potentials the realization of which is our perfection as a species, as individuals we possess some potentials more fully than others.

We have not only a shared human nature but also an individual nature that embraces something not completely shared by all. Our general human nature, encompassing many capacities, means that our perfection lies in many-sided development. But our distinct nature as individuals biases some potentials over others, and we realize our particular character by expressing our "own nature," following the "inward forces" affecting us specifically. Mill's case against the ethical relevance of the physical order (or disorder) of nature does not preclude him from relying on human nature in his moral defense of individual liberty and his case against the subjection of women. For that matter, Mill's very claim that it would be wrong to take physical nature as an ethical guide depends on his understanding of human nature, for a morality imitative of physical nature would do violence to what is best and most promising in human nature.

Mill's general defense of liberty depends in part on the moral implications of human nature, as does his more specific defense of women's liberation. The problem with enforcing social roles, like gender roles, is that no one who is coerced into a role, or who passively accepts an inherited role, can live a life of conviction expressed through conscious and deliberate choice. Only choice can generate conviction. Living by our choices both *is* our human nature and is what best allows us to discover and express our own nature. On Mill's understanding of human nature, it matters that the roles constituting our life express our nature; coercing half the population to fill a particular role pays no heed to whether, in an individual case, the role suits one's nature. Because deliberate choice is part of our nature, and because by it we are most likely to realize our individual nature, enforced social roles prevent us from realizing our best development. Raised to inhabit only a stipulated social role, women, Mill says, receive an "unnatural upbringing." Better to raise women in accordance with their human capacities, and to let women, like men, choose their own way of life, and "feel the liberal interest natural to any cultivated human being, in the great transactions which took place around them, and in which they might be called on to take a part."[34] To develop their distinctively human capacities, women must be assured the right to choose their vocation rather than be compelled to fill an ascribed role.

John Stuart Mill's ethic of fulfillment suggests what "fit" comes to mean in a liberal democratic age. No longer a correspondence between individual nature and fixed social orders or places, it is rather something we each might seek and realize. To find our fit, we have to shake off the despotic yoke of societal expectations, know ourselves, find our own path, and live by the light of our own choices. This is not to say that whatever we choose is right because we chose it. Something great is at stake in a real choice: choices can go wrong, terribly and irretrievably so. Nothing prevents us from choosing unwisely, or from losing our way in the comfort of convention. Yet the possibility remains that each might find his or her fit and so realize fulfillment.

Fulfillment, so it seems, is open to all. It carries no formal prerequisites, no legal status or titles, no ascribed traits like gender. Yet in practice it is decisively foreclosed to many, at least in Mill's honest account. Everyone will not have an equal share in the highest human capacities, nor will all have the upbringing, the opportunity, or the fortitude to realize his or her individuality. On the contrary, Mill's ideal is best realized by the rare heroic type, the few "who are the salt of the earth."[35] Perhaps Mill's effort to describe the components of well-being was not idiosyncratic—progressive liberal democracy needs, for its pride, self-confidence, and direction, more than the project of combating inherited injustices. It also needs a goal, a model of character and well-being that it distinctively makes possible. Yet democracy exerts an irresistible tendency to universalize well-being, to affirm that human fulfillment does not by necessity belong only to the few, however salty. One expression of this tendency is seen in Betty Friedan's feminism, which extends the promise of fulfillment to the roles of everyday life. Friedan holds up careers as *the* singular source of fulfillment in modern life. Yet unwittingly inheriting the frailty of the Protestant ethic, she seems unable to connect the great ideals she imposes on careers with the concrete experience of work.

7

Friedan's Careerism

Almost a hundred years after Mill, Betty Friedan published a blistering critique of the social and economic confinement of women that animated Mill's essay. On all sides, her claims are more extreme than Mill's: she castigates domestic work as beneath the capacities of a moderately capable person, and she upholds paid careers as the singular and most promising source of human fulfillment. Paid careers, she holds, are more fitting than a life relegated to the domicile; they make good on the promise of fulfillment by connecting people to important public purposes and developing their higher capacities. The medium through which we work out purposes that are distinctively *ours,* careers offer us a rich opportunity to express our authentic self. Friedan's is a demanding ideal of fit—one that asks much not only of individuals but also of the world of work. Yet she seems not to recognize the weight of her demands, blind to the gap between her own expectations for work and the working life surrounding her.

This gap rendered Friedan's ideals of fulfillment vulnerable. Perhaps for this reason, in later additions to her original 1963 book, Friedan turns away from the promise of fulfillment through work and focuses more on the plain fact that work is chosen.[1] Her early work reflected the hope that choice and fit could go together: free to choose, individuals would locate fitting careers. But in an essay published twenty years later, the cool lessons of experience seem to have suppressed her original hope that choice could be placed in the service of fulfillment, she extols choice for its own sake and implicitly gives up on the promise of fitting work.

Critique of the Domestic Ideal

Friedan's argument against restricting women to domestic work does not depend on the economic importance of working and earning. She does not invoke the need for two incomes to maintain middle-class family comforts. For Friedan, the ideal of domesticity is itself deeply flawed. Because its defects are keenly felt even among the advantaged—affluent, married women with children living in comfortable suburban homes—Friedan argues that the ideal must be profoundly wrong at its core. Over several hundred spirited pages Friedan claims that healthy and capable human beings cannot be said to fit a domestic role. At points Friedan goes as far as to claim that domestic work—caring for home and family—is work not suited to any human being. In light of these claims, Friedan does not argue simply for extending the scope of free choice, as if whatever persons might freely choose would be for that reason just. Instead she holds free choice to be important because by choice we are more likely to find work that fits. For Friedan, the claims of human nature support the moral importance of choice.

For Friedan, the ideal of traditional womanhood elevates women's sexual role into a life role, and thus it fails to offer the sort of work that might call forth a woman's full capacities. The problem with the domestic ideal is not only that it limits women to "one passion, one role, one occupation" but also that this singular role is itself too limited; it lacks stimulating and engaging work.[2] Housework, in Friedan's view, calls on few energies and demands little creativity. Yet in the absence of any demanding purpose, Friedan believes, housewives devote themselves unreasonably to housework and spend far more time than is really required to keep a house tidy and working well. The attempt to make homemaking a full-time career prompts women, in Friedan's observation, to spend as much time doing housework as people did before the introduction of such labor-saving devices as washing machines and electric freezers, by doing more work than is necessary.

Friedan tells, for instance, of a thirty-six-year-old bachelor who, after asserting in a letter to a local paper that housewives managed their time poorly, was challenged to take over the care of a home and four young children for several days; on the first day, he completed the cooking and cleaning necessary for a week.[3] "A baked potato is not as big as the world," Friedan asserts, "and vacuuming the living room floor—with or without makeup—is not work that takes enough thought or energy to challenge any woman's full capacity." In a home filled with modern appliances, with food needs served by convenient supermarkets instead of backyard gardens, domestic work does not draw on very large mental capacities, she insists. The domestic role requires that women remain untalented, and is suited to the "feeble-minded," such as "8 year-olds" or even the "mentally retarded."[4]

When human beings of potential and talent try to conform themselves to a role that cannot use their abilities, they become stunted and eventually deformed, Friedan argues. Instead of providing work that fits women's abilities and develops their talents, the domestic ideal asks women for a "premature commitment to one role." This commitment, partly encouraged, partly enforced, allows women, Friedan says, to "evade" real choices about how to structure their lives. By this evasion, women remain immature because they avoid the risks of real choice, such as the risk that they will have chosen wrongly, or that they will fail to succeed in a chosen role. Accepting an ascribed role that draws on little talent also means that women will not share in the sense of mastery and fulfillment that comes through successful commitment to a chosen role. Inhabiting a role that did not use their abilities or draw out their potential resulted, Friedan says, in a pervasive sense of emptiness among housewives in the 1950s. This desperate emptiness Friedan calls "the problem that has no name."[5]

Friedan considers several possible solutions to this sense of emptiness. One solution is that women focus on romantic and sexual pleasures. But these, Friedan argues, usually fail because they cannot satisfy needs that are not primarily romantic or sexual. Of women who turn to sex as a source of fulfillment, Friedan asks, "are these married women putting into their insatiable sexual search the aggressive energies which the feminine mystique forbids them to use for larger human purposes? Are they using sex or sexual fantasy to fill needs that are not sexual?" Friedan does not contemplate the distinction between sex and love, or consider the possibility that devotion to sex alone aspires to something less than romance. She assumes, rather, that a manic turn to sex for complete satisfaction represents a diversion motivated by the lack of serious purpose embodied in women's traditional domestic role. Besides sex, shopping and the activities connected with consumerism present other possible solutions to a sense of emptiness, and Friedan argues that marketers knowingly exploit the housewife's feeling of emptiness. Although Friedan concedes that women "can be given the sense of identity, purpose, creativity, the self-realization, even the sexual joy they lack—by the buying of things," this sense is ultimately a false solution.[6] Because few find real purpose in what they purchase, consumerism fails to fill the emptiness that motivates it.

These possible solutions neglect the activity that seems most likely to lend purpose and meaning to the domestic role: raising and educating children. But Friedan says that tending to children and home is not sufficient to give women a serious purpose—that activities connected with child rearing constitute only half of life, not life's whole. As advertisers discovered through market research, she points out, "American women have complex needs which home-and-family, love-and-children, cannot fill." While Friedan believes the "problem that has no name" is pervasive, she also knows that many women welcome a commitment to the domestic role. They suffer, she argues, from false consciousness. Subjective contentment is one thing, and may come from conformity with received convention. A fulfilling adult life is another. Conceding that not all housewives are unhappy, Friedan argues that "happiness is not the same thing as the aliveness of being fully used . . . Housework, no matter how it is expanded to fill the time available, can hardly use the abilities of a woman of average or normal human intelligence." When women attempt to reconcile themselves to their domestic role, they evade their growth and refuse to grow up; barred from serious intellectual or creative endeavor, they may suffer, in their perpetual state of immaturity, a sort of "human deformity."[7]

As women's dedication to the domestic role is bad for themselves, frustrating some and stunting all, so too it is bad for their children. In contrast with earlier Progressives who extolled educated motherhood, Friedan indicates that full-time mothering involves problems stemming from maternal overprotection.[8] Not one to suggest a conflict between parents' fulfillment and children's needs, Friedan suggests that children suffer from the obsessive attention and overprotection of mothers constrained to the domestic role. Shorn of independent purposes, these mothers attempt to live vicariously through their children; when frustrated in this attempt, they struggle to control their children, and deprive the children of the autonomy that they themselves lack. The net effect is that children may suffer an array of psychological problems. Friedan asserts, "Most of the problems now being treated in child-guidance clinics are solved only when mothers are helped to develop autonomous interests of their own, and no longer need to fill their emotional needs through their children."[9] As the constant and vigilant attention of full-time mothers toward their children is bad for both, Friedan suggests that what is good for mothers is also good for children.

But what, on this analysis, is good for mothers—or for women in general? The problem with the feminine mystique, on Friedan's account, is not simply that domesticity is coerced or unchosen, not even only that it makes some women unhappy, but that it prevents them from becoming "fully human," or from exercising their distinctively human capacities. Citing a "hierarchy of needs in man," Friedan states that the feminine mystique prevents women from developing their higher human capacities by recognizing no need "higher than the need for love or sexual satisfaction." Women need to use their full capacities, meaning that they need to make the choices that would give them a "personal purpose stretching into the future." They need, like all humans, "to grow and to realize one's full potential."[10] Not by serving others in the family, not through consumption, not through sex, but only by satisfying these human needs will women be fulfilled as individuals. The feminine mystique is wrong because it fails to recognize and answer the claims of human nature.

Solving Emptiness through Expressive Work

Friedan holds that these claims of human nature find recognition not in the family or domesticity but in work. "Women," she says, "as well as men, can only find their identity in work that uses their full capacities. A woman cannot find her identity through others— her husband, her children. She cannot find it in the dull routine of housework."[11] Friedan does not settle for the practical point that the right to earn would diminish the leverage that money gives husbands over their wives, and would therefore give women a more equal footing with respect to men. The importance of work, for Friedan, lies not in the way the "power of earning," in Mill's phrase, gives women a basic security and dignity, but rather in the way the activity of work in a career brings fulfillment.[12] Work is the solution to emptiness. The expectation is that the purposes served through work will be aligned with one's personal purposes.

Not just any jobs will serve Friedan's ideal of work, but only those that allow individuals to express and pursue a purpose that is both personal and recognized socially as important. Only "creative work . . . that contributes to the human community," "honored and useful work," "work important to the world," and "responsible work" that fits one's "actual capacity" will provide the fulfillment lacking in the domestic role. Work in this ideal is not a burden to be tolerated for what it provides; it is not simply a difficult means of survival or the way to a decent paycheck. As an antidote to the housewife's problems, work must fit people in a way housework and domesticity, on Friedan's description, cannot. Although work in this ideal requires sustained commitment and effort, the commitment is elicited for the work itself, not for the sake of something outside the work, such as money, comfort, family, leisure. Work contains its own reason. As the solution to emptiness, work assumes the roles of religion and philosophy. Work has a "human significance," Friedan says, "not merely as the means of biological survival, but as the giver of self and the transcender of self, as the creator of human identity and human evolution."[13] Work is the foundry of our identity, for Friedan. We can be, in the fullest sense, only if we work—and if our work fits us in the way Friedan expects. This is why careers are the solution to the problem that has no name.

Friedan's criticism of the domestic role for women is ultimately a claim about the sort of work men *and* women, because of their human nature, justly deserve. Like men, she argues, women deserve work that recognizes and expresses their distinctly human capacities. Choice is crucial, but only to the extent that choice leads individuals to find work that fits them. In her original 1963 text, Friedan in effect claimed that the traditional domestic role is not worthy of being chosen, although some may choose it.[14] She deplores efforts to accommodate women to the traditional role or to educate women so that they will be more likely to choose it. On the contrary, she insists that "Drastic steps must be taken to re-educate women" so they feel the urgency of escaping the confines set by the feminine mystique.[15]

Fulfillment Frustrated: Critics of Work in the 1950s

Friedan believed that careers would fit the abilities of women in general, and, more important, that they would call forth expressive capacities and provide a personal purpose. As the source of personal identity and highest purposes, careers would lend meaning and a sense of fullness to women's lives. In her emphasis on developing "identity" and meaning through *personal* purpose and creativity, Friedan gave voice to the romantic hope that work in the real world could fit people not only in a basic way but ideally. Such optimism is not unique to Friedan. It underlines, if in more temperate form, the general promise of work. The ideal of perfect fit gives support, as we saw, to the work ethic: if work is the basis of our identity and fulfillment, then it makes sense to dedicate ourselves to our jobs.

Of course, the assembly of expectations Friedan held for careers—where they would contain profound personal purpose, even a reason for existence—stands some distance from the lived experience of work. Friedan's analysis focused on the frustrated aspirations of only the most advantaged: educated, middle-class, married, suburban, white women. She overlooked the lot of working women who worked in mere jobs, as she also neglected the struggles of black women.[16] Hers was a middle-class analysis that looked not to the real experience of work but to the ideal promise of careers. Yet Friedan also failed to notice that this ideal was elusive even for men. At the same time that Friedan held up paid careers as the antidote to women's emptiness, other observers of the 1950s workplace found little to celebrate. Critics such as C. Wright Mills, David Riesman, William H. Whyte, and Daniel Bell found work not only in factories but also in offices and large corporations deficient in many of the same ways Friedan identified with respect to household work. In their accounts, work provided few opportunities for creative self-expression and brought little meaning to the lives of workers.

Contrary to Friedan's hopes, salaried white-collar jobs in the 1950s usually did not sustain one's spirit, according to C. Wright Mills. Although white-collar work avoided the drudgery of factory work, in Mills's view it was alienating just the same. If softer in its physical demands, white-collar work could not meet the ideal of craftsmanship because it developed few ties between producer and product and did not elicit a high degree of skill. And salaried office work offered no intrinsic connection between work and one's life outside work. White-collar workers, Mills claimed, "must accept their work as meaningless in itself, perform it with more or less disgruntlement, and seek meanings elsewhere."[17] While Mills addressed midlevel white-collar work, in William H. Whyte's view, even executive-level work could not provide the opportunity for creative accomplishment through work.

At the executive level, professional work in large organizations placed cooperation and working smoothly with others ahead of personal initiative and individual creativity. In Whyte's view, the effort to adapt to the needs of a large organization by becoming a "practical, team-player" and developing the loyalty of an "organization man" could not fully overcome the "conflict between the individual as he is and as he wishes to be, and the role he is called upon to play."[18] For executives, work was the center of life, and it gave them scarcely any time or energy for family, civic engagements, or creative avocations. While work consumed much time and energy, Whyte reported, executives of the 1950s lacked much control over their destiny or integrity. Vulnerable to being transferred and burdened by the necessity of pleasing others, executives, for all their power, lacked a certain control over their own lives and their own self-expression. In Whyte's view, individuals in large organizations are under the constant pressure of selling—not only selling a product but also selling their own personality. Making allies, cultivating contacts, building one's reputation within a firm all require a manner of easygoing fellowship. As gregariousness becomes more contrived, it diminishes one's sense of individual integrity and lessens the opportunity for individual accomplishment. Many corporate executives, Whyte notes, "point out that when one's job is inextricably involved with others, the sense of individual creativity and the satisfaction of being able to deliver a tied-up package of achievement is hard to come by."[19] On Whyte's description, even the executive's work in the 1950s lacked the sense of personal accomplishment promised by Friedan's ideal of paid work in a career.

The requirements of working smoothly with others and of treating "everyone as a customer who is always right" contributed to the rise of a new type of American worker in the 1950s, according to David Riesman. Radar-sensitive to the expectations of others, these individuals abjured any internalized ethic of achievement and duty.[20] Although they often asked more from work than decent pay and status, they nonetheless found that work could not meet their aspirations, in Riesman's view, for it posed too many obstacles to self-directed action. For Riesman, the necessity of pleasing others ("glad-handing") and contriving a personable appearance ("false personalization") meant that work could not supply an extensive arena for autonomous activity. Against this reality, Riesman recommended relaxing high expectations for work and suggested that it be viewed simply as a source of livelihood rather than as a place of personal fulfillment. Most jobs will not elicit people's "emotional and creative energies," Riesman observed, and—following the example of Thoreau (who was a surveyor) or William Carlos Williams (a doctor)—he hoped people would be more willing "to justify their work primarily by its paycheck." Not work but play, he said, offered the best opportunity to develop "competence in the art of living." The expanded leisure time made possible by industrial production offered the best opportunities for self-direction through fulfilling, creative endeavor, in Riesman's view; attempts to "personalize, emotionalize, and moralize the machine process" would not make work any more fulfilling.[21]

Other observers of the workplace were less ready to accept such fatalism. Noting that work had "always stood at the center of moral consciousness," Daniel Bell argued that more attention should be directed to making work more satisfying.[22] Work, along with religion, he said, is for human beings the chief way of guarding against a debilitating fear of death and mobilizing creative energies to both master nature and develop self-discipline. Yet motive to work in America, he noted, comes from the allure of consumption. This is inferior, in Bell's view, to working for the sake of something internal to the work process itself. Nor is it sufficient, he thought, if aspects of the work environment tangential to the actual work are satisfying, such as the opportunity to socialize with coworkers; Bell hoped that satisfactions gained through the work process itself might be sufficient reason to work, and enough to motivate a will to work. Meeting this ideal, he said, would mean challenging the concept of efficiency and structuring the division of labor with the understanding that, for the worker, a job "must not only feed his body; it must sustain his spirit."[23]

These critics suggest that the problems Friedan identified with the domestic role existed for workers in general—even for those in careers. Work, at least the paid work that in fact surrounded Friedan, could not provide the fulfillment and sense of purpose that Friedan expected. Her ideal of perfectly fulfilling work indeed raises the standard so high that nearly all work will fall short. By motivating a frustration with work in general, the promise of perfect fulfillment deprives us of a nuanced understanding of how work can be good and meaningful. Perhaps work does not need to be the central or primary source of meaning and purpose for work in a more modest sense to be meaningful and purposive. For instance, rather than expecting work alone to be the "giver of self and the transcender of self," it might be more appropriate to focus on the sort of meaning and satisfaction work might actually provide. We might attend more carefully to the internal goods work can offer, and the requirements of realizing those goods. The contemporary economy of labor contains powerful pressures to separate the conceptual part of work (thinking through what needs to be done, and how it best ought to be done) and the execution of tasks; some, usually managers, do all the conceptual tasks, and other workers are charged with executing what they have conceived. Attending to the real possibility of repairing this divide, of integrating conceptual tasks with the execution of tasks, also matters.[24] But when confronting actual work, the ideal of perfect fulfillment leads to a disappointment that masks the possibilities of work founded in a more grounded understanding of how it might fit individuals. For Friedan, the extreme expectations she placed on work led her, later, to abandon the promise of work.

Pay and Choice

The frustrated promise of fulfillment led Friedan in the end to a much lower standard. In the 1973 epilogue to her original book, Friedan turns away from her earlier concern with the intrinsic importance of work.[25] Instead she focuses on the importance of monetary pay and nominal choice. As the ideal of expressive, purposeful work seemed out of reach, Friedan in the end focuses on the goal that work be socially recognized, and few signs of social recognition are more persuasive than pay. Moreover, earning can free one from relationships in which economic dependence underlines general dependence. The ability to earn is therefore more central to a feminism that focuses on equal power rather than personal fulfillment. Friedan retreats from the ideal of fulfillment and instead emphasizes the instrumental importance of jobs for money. Pay, not a good fit, is the mark of good work. As Friedan states: "Equality and human dignity are not possible for women if they are not able to earn . . . [for] very few women can afford to ignore the elementary economic facts of life. Only economic independence can free a woman to marry for love, not for status or financial support, or to leave a loveless, intolerable, humiliating marriage, or to eat, dress, rest, and move if she plans not to marry."[26]

The focus on pay seems to offer a more practical goal than fulfillment, and to better recognize the material importance of money and basic security. But now the practical importance of earning supplies the meaning, the purpose that animates Friedan's case for careers. While pay has its place, it seems to displace the broader concerns that so infused Friedan's earlier writing. As the only purpose of work and career, pay may even introduce a "mode of valuation" that crowds out other values, like fulfillment, that speak to the larger meaning of work.[27] Market norms of buying and selling, in which each serves the other but also tries to get the best of the other, encourage people to take earning as the source of motivation for working, and to regard their relations with others as capable of being dissolved should they find a better deal elsewhere. By encouraging people to work for pay, market norms discourage other sorts of valuation, such as the familial and affective norms that motivate much household labor, such as parenting. Elevating pay, without attention to the more general promise of work, overprivileges money as a source of both valuation and motivation.

This is one reason choice can be such an attractive standard: it helps avoid the ideal expectations that Friedan originally imposed on careers, and it reaches beyond the strictly practical standard of pay. Like Mill, Friedan, in her original writing, emphasizes choice, and they both defend the importance of choice on the grounds that choice is more likely to lead to work suitable to one's capacities. Yet in a 1983 essay appended to later editions of *The Feminine Mystique*, Friedan retreats from the force of her earliest writing. She reverses herself by asserting that there is nothing wrong with domestic work—or any other work—so long as it is chosen. "*Chosen* motherhood is the real liberation," she says. "The *choice* to have a child makes the whole experience of motherhood different, and the choice to be generative in other ways can at last be made, and is being made by many women now."[28] Here Friedan gives up on any standard that might orient or guide choice. All that matters is that work is chosen. By the 1980s, Friedan no longer envisions a society that offers men and women work that contains developmental and expressive possibilities; instead she lauds a society in which every role is the result of an individual's choice.

Mill, too, as we saw, regarded the erosion of ascribed roles and the extension of free choice as an unambiguous improvement. The ethic of freedom and the dissolution of aristocratic assumptions meant that restricting all women to one role seemed anomalous, out of date, and unjust. Women's subjection, Mill noted, is a "relic of the past . . . and must necessarily disappear."[29] Perhaps all roles not of our making and choosing lack justification and must of necessity disappear. The argument against women's traditional roles can be seen as part of a larger case against all roles beyond our choosing that entail obligations. Each individual, not society or social understandings, should define the roles he or she lives out. Yet Mill did not defend choice entirely for its own sake, nor did he think that choice alone confers justice on the roles that are chosen. Choice achieves moral significance, in Mill's analysis, because living according to our deliberate choice is part of our nature and because we are more likely to find a role suited to our nature by making our own choice than in another way. The value of choice is not freestanding but depends on the possibility that there are valuable things to choose from. For Mill, the status of free choice is partly derived from the value of roles that fit our nature and express it. If choice about work is important partly for the sake of achieving the right fit with work, then Friedan's original emphasis on fulfilling work is not displaced by her later emphasis on choice alone.

Friedan's movement from fitting work to chosen work—from an idealized expectation to a very modest one—suggests the danger that the ideal of fitting work imposes. By setting a standard that is out of reach, the ideal of perfect fit risks losing all critical leverage. For her part, Friedan forgot to ask what her ideal demanded of the world of work—and thus neglected what sort of answer work might offer. She packed everything into her ideal: expressive and developmental fulfillment, social recognition, good pay. In the end she concedes all these in favor of simple choice. But along the way she overlooks the middle ground, the place where fit might be found, if only incompletely. As a result, she ends up slighting the very promise that originally animated her critique. And in so doing, she ends up with the sociologists of midcentury who examined work in America.

Each in his own way—Mills, Whyte, Riesman, Bell—believed that the traditional Protestant ethic was insufficient by the 1950s to motivate or justify any sort of work ethic. Without the internalized guides of religion and achievement, Riesman said, work was a discipline that seemed "against the grain of man's nature." For Bell, the "new appetite for work" (reflected in Friedan's celebration of careers) left unaddressed the connection between work and the human spirit. And for her part, Friedan mimicked some of the weaknesses of the original Protestant ethic by failing to attend to the particular ways in which abstract ideals like free expression or full development might connect concretely with the practices of work. She expected that work could supply meaning and purpose, yet she did not bother to say how. To do so would require attending to the particular goods to be found within the working life. Realizing these goods involves a kind of fulfillment, though one more incomplete than the careers Friedan imagined would offer.

8

Work as a Practice

Both the Protestant work ethic and the ideal of perfect fit in Betty Friedan's careerism invest ordinary work with great purpose, yet neither gives an adequate account of how such purposes connect with the activity of work. In the Protestant account, faith enjoins diligent work in a settled path. But the activity of work itself does not inform a deeper, more abiding, or more authentic faith. The great purpose given by faith and the travail of work stand apart: faith imposes purpose on work, almost regardless of what one works at. Only after accepting faith does everyday work attain such a status that it appears worthy of devotion for reasons that extend beyond what it produces in this life. The ideal of a fulfilling career stands as a secular equivalent to the Protestant ethic, in the sense that it grounds a kind of commitment to the working life. But like the Protestant ethic, this ideal fails to connect with the activity of work. The absence of such a connection led Friedan to conclude eventually that choice alone—rather than fulfillment—was what mattered. Thus the promise of work that so powerfully informed *The Feminine Mystique* in 1963 was abandoned, as if to concede to Mill that fulfillment is too demanding to be democratized. Can an ideal of fulfillment be connected to the experience of work? What does it mean to fit our work so well that it is truly worthy of devotion? The promise implicit in the work ethic itself depends on the answer.

Some argue that the promise of work depends on connecting it more explicitly with the common good or social needs, on the one hand, and with intrinsic meaning, on the other. Through a series of interpretive vignettes, Robert Bellah and the coauthors of *Habits of the Heart* illustrate the difficulties of sustaining and justifying a commitment to work in commercial society.[1] Even consuming and challenging careers—the central source of fulfillment for Friedan—ultimately fail to elicit deep and worthwhile commitment. One representative character named Brian, for instance, defines his identity through his success as a high-level corporate manager. While very devoted to his work, his dedication is not so much to his work as to himself. Continuously evaluating what he gets out of work, Brian must always stand somewhat apart from the activity of his work. Work is worthy of commitment, Bellah argues, when it shapes our character and directs our efforts toward purposes larger than ourselves. The traditional approach to careers, in Bellah's view, is more selfish than social—even the helping professions, he says, too often lack the inner meaning and external connection to larger social purposes that is characteristic of callings. In another vignette, Bellah tells of an academic psychologist whose commitment to her work is tempered by the doubt that it contributes only to those "who have been in therapy and talk like psychologists." Other professional work, such as lawyering, also suffers, he finds: the "intrinsic meaninglessness in any larger moral or social context" of such work makes it unworthy of great commitment and incapable of producing lasting rewards for its practitioners.[2]

The Common Good

Bellah and colleagues submit the individuals interviewed to an intense form of scrutiny that one imagines few could survive without revealing some incoherence in the nature of their commitment—as if the moral life could be characterized by easy justification. In any case, few could fully explain the basis of their commitment to academic observers, just as few academics could successfully discern the true nature of the commitments individuals live out. Yet Bellah's deepest aim is not simply to criticize individuals, as if some sort of moral decision or psychological shift on an individual level might result in a deeper and more lasting commitment. Instead he intends to evaluate critically the moral conceptions prevalent in the culture and their relation to the broader commercial society. The stories collected thus stand as invitations to more deeply assess both the organization of work and the understandings that market economies subtly but strongly encourage among individuals. Market rationality exercises a formidable influence, in Bellah's view, by encouraging individuals to consistently evaluate the bargain implicit in their work, and therefore to stand apart from their work. At the same time, the elaborate division of industrial labor and the constraints of market competition occlude the relation of work to social welfare. Tempering market rationality to enlighten our sense of nonmonetary rewards and to shape work roles that make a more direct social contribution is necessary if work is to be worthy of individual commitment, Bellah and colleagues argue.

One solution to the thin commitment work elicits, on this argument, lies in connecting work more profoundly with the social good: "The calling of each is a contribution to the good of all," Bellah insists.[3] The contribution that work makes, not only to one's own support but to the larger world, is a critical part of its meaning. The effect of one's work on the larger society is a source of both work's obligatory character and the pride and dignity that we associate with the working life. When we fit our work from a social perspective, we optimize our contribution to society. Social fit and social contribution are undeniable parts of work's satisfaction and meaning. But how work affects those who do it, independent of the contribution they make, is another question. It is one thing to say that contribution matters; it is another to hold that social contribution alone warrants a more complete devotion to work. This demands an uncommon sort of selflessness. Moreover, it is a sort of selflessness that we should hope remains uncommon so long as we prize individuality and democratic pride. Grounding a conception of the calling entirely on work's service to the common good leaves individuals and their distinct claims and aspirations too much to the side. It speaks to the social fit we saw in Plato's *Republic* but leaves personal fit entirely unaddressed.

Indeed, even Bellah and coauthors agree that the activity of work ideally possesses an intrinsic value that accrues solely to those who do it (rather than simply a social value that benefits the community). Work possesses a "meaning and value in itself, not just in the output or profit that results from it." This intrinsic value is what distinguishes callings from careers. Yet other than stressing self-abnegation, they say little about the sources of this intrinsic value: "In a calling one gives oneself to learning and practicing activities that in turn define the self and enter into the shape of its character."[4] *Habits of the Heart* also neglects to address the difficulties involved in squaring what is intrinsically rewarding with what is socially useful. Social contribution and intrinsic value are distinct. Pile drivers may contribute greatly to the common good but not realize much inner meaning in the process of the work. River guides may find important rewards internal to the work yet offer less to society at large. As Mill and Friedan held up developmental and expressive fulfillment, as the Protestant ethic held up faith, so Bellah and colleagues exalt the common good and intrinsic meaning. But they, too, do not specify how these ends might be connected to the activity of work. For instance, they do not say how we might understand the intrinsic meaning of work, such that it could on its own merit a deeper commitment. Is inner meaning, in a secular context, simply a synonym for pleasure, and if so, is devotion to work any different than devotion to money, which is obviously useful for securing pleasures?

The Practice of Work

Alasdair MacIntyre's concept of a "practice" helps explain how work might possess an inner meaning. For his part, MacIntyre is more concerned with elucidating the meaning of virtue than with explaining the intrinsic rewards of work. Indeed, MacIntyre is pessimistic about the possibilities for work in modern commercial societies—and for that matter is pessimistic about modern society in general. Yet his account of practices has more application in the modern world than MacIntyre is wont to concede. It explains with some precision the way in which work, and activities more generally, might be experienced as intrinsically worthwhile or fulfilling. One can accept the account of practices without endorsing MacIntyre's broader antimodern stance. According to MacIntyre, a practice includes several elements: first, it involves an activity that is coherent, complex, cooperative, and socially established; second, the activity motivates its participants through goods that are internal to the activity and gained through the effort to achieve excellence at the activity; and third, dedication to the activity extends the capacity to achieve excellence and intellectually grasp the goods involved in the activity.[5] What would it mean for work to be a practice, and can the ideal of work as a practice be aligned with what society needs? Considering each of the three elements of a practice in turn will help elucidate the way practices relate to work.

Most work is "socially established and cooperative." Work usually situates the worker within a community of others defined minimally by their market relations—networks of coworkers, employers, buyers, and sellers form the cooperative world of work. It is less clear that every form of work is sufficiently complex to qualify as a practice; much of the most mundane and repetitive work might fail to qualify on this count alone. Whether this is so hangs on what is implied by the term *complex*. If we take it to refer to a variety and combination of discrete tasks, and to the conception and execution, then much work will not qualify as complex enough to count as a practice. Work that involves the repetitive performance of the same simple task, or that requires solely execution, like telemarketing or assembly-line jobs, would fall short of this standard. Whether work is complex enough to qualify as a practice in any particular case would require a sensitive appreciation of the details of the work. Even work sometimes thought mundane can turn out to be surprisingly complicated; tasks such as waiting tables and driving taxis, for instance, require much conceptual and organizational effort, as anyone who has attempted to time the serving of many meals or to pick the best rush-hour route knows.[6] Complexity is central to practices, but for work to count as a practice depends on something more.

Internal Standards

Practices are also distinguished from activities more generally by the fact that they possess standards and purposes that are internal to the meaning of the activity. To see this, consider how the same formal activity—banking—might be or not be a practice, depending on the sense of purpose and the sorts of standards that regulate the activity. Banking, like most work, aims to generate an economic return. But for banking to be a practice, it must have purposes that are specific to it. Profits, after all, might be realized in many other ways: making refrigerators, flying airplanes, writing sitcoms. What defines the activity of banking is not the aim of profits per se, but rather the aim of making profits *while* adhering to certain standards that are themselves unrelated to profit. In this case, the standards will differ depending on whether we are talking about merchant banking, consumer lending, investment banking, and so on; but it is the particular purpose of the activity, not the general aim of profits, that would allow banking to be conceived of and carried out as a practice. The purpose of a loan officer is to make good loans—to lend in a manner that ensures the loans will be put to good use and will be repaid. Profit is a by-product of this characteristic purpose. Only those purposes that are internal to the activity of banking itself give rise to particular standards by which those who perform the activity are judged, and only they make it possible to speak of some bankers as better than others when all are equally good at netting profits. Within the context of a practice, excellence or advancement is measured neither against market rewards nor with reference to other standards external to the activity itself; excellence is gauged against standards of quality internal to the activity that are taught and enforced by the community of practitioners.

Activities with internal standards are social in that the standards defining them are transmitted (and transformed) through time by the community of those dedicated to the practice. Looking to crafts and professions for illustration, Bellah says, "Committing oneself to becoming a 'good' carpenter, craftsman, doctor, scientist, or artist anchors the self within a community practicing carpentry, medicine, or art. It connects the self to those who teach, exemplify, and judge these skills."[7] The socially established and cooperative nature of practices means that a practice is never an activity of one's own invention; rather its aims and its norms are held, taught, and enforced by those who, because of their common dedication to the practice, form a particular sort of community. The community defined by a practice may be wide and at the margins include all those dedicated to the purposes and standards internal to a practice; in the case of sports, for instance, coaches, athletes, former players, and even spectators constitute this sort of community.

Many activities from the world of work have internal standards. Only a few things, after all, are so simple that they cannot admit to being done better or worse. But practices are more than techniques. The difference between a practice and any activity involving technical competence can be appreciated by considering the goods that are internal to the work. To count as a practice, an activity must not only have purposes that define it specifically but also offer certain goods or rewards to those who devote themselves to and achieve some proficiency in the activity. MacIntyre argues that these rewards can be gained only through engagement in the practice itself; there is no alternate method of realizing them. The classic external goods—fame, power, and money—might be had in many ways; as such, they are not internal to any particular activity. They are external also in another sense: they are not constitutive of one's character. They are to be used, deployed, invested, enjoyed, and as such are plenty desirable. However, good though they are, they are different from internal goods.

Internal Goods

To clarify the nature of internal goods, MacIntyre considers the example of teaching a child chess. Since the internal rewards of chess are not evident to a child unfamiliar with the game, one might offer candy as an inducement to play. But the good central to playing chess is not candy—it is a "certain highly particular kind of analytic skill, strategic imagination and competitive intensity."[8] The hope is that as the child becomes more proficient, the necessity for an external reward will diminish and the internal goods will come to supply sufficient motivation for playing. Here MacIntyre focuses on the habits of mind that chess inculcates. These, and not an external good like candy, are what should motivate individuals to pursue the practice, for they are the true point or end of the practice. To speak of internal goods as rewards or sources of motivation is appropriate in the sense that internal goods involve pleasure. But satisfaction or pleasure is not principally what they are about. The point of the internal goods associated with chess is not simply the generic pleasure the game supplies—pleasure as a desirable psychic state is available in many different ways, and a drug might effectively supply pleasure without the trouble of learning something demanding like chess. The internal goods of chess are abilities, the exercise of which brings a particular kind of pleasure.

In this respect, internal goods are distinct from whatever psychic reward one happens to perceive. They are developed capacities that facilitate proficiency or success in a practice. As a sense of rhythm is a good internal to musical practice, so are coordination and body awareness internal to athletic practices. Relaxed intensity is internal to meditative practice, as practical judgment is internal to the practice of law. Internal goods are goods of character that make a claim on our identity and give definition to life—they shape who we are and make us persons of a particular sort. We might describe the internal goods of a practice such as portrait painting, to take another of MacIntyre's examples, as a collection of discrete abilities: a sense of color, an understanding of composition and light. But these are subservient to a more central good, an ability to cast a person's likeness in a way that reveals something of their essential character. And even this good is in service to the chief good conveyed by the practice, which is leading a "certain kind of life," or living out life *"as a painter."*[9] To be sure, not every practice will give definition to the whole of life, but these examples illustrate the central feature of internal goods: they do not reduce to enjoyment or pleasure. Instead, they are transformative goods. Practices, and the internal goods they convey, are not merely performed or enacted but are *lived.*

If many activities have internal standards, fewer perhaps have internal goods. Many tasks—trimming lawns, washing dishes, copying papers, operating machinery—cannot in themselves be understood as practices, though they do require technical competence. These activities have standards and purposes appropriate to them, but they do not offer significant internal goods to those who perform them. Still, any of these tasks may be part of a larger activity that constitutes a practice of sorts: mowing may be part of the practice of farming, washing dishes may be part of sustaining a home, copying pages part of composing a book. These discrete activities do not convey internal goods on their own, but when situated in a larger context they might count as practices.[10]

Work and Internal Goods

In advanced industrial economies, work is not designed for the purpose of conveying internal goods. It is designed, of course, for productivity and profit. The conflict between the incentives that shape work under capitalism and the goods that make work fulfilling causes some to think that there is no hope for work in the modern world, short of a radical restructuring of the economy through a kind of social revolution. Harry Braverman, for instance, guided by Marx's insights about the logic of capitalism, holds that nothing less than a social revolution that returns the control of the process of work to workers themselves will fundamentally improve the quality of work. The pursuit of profit, which is sewn into the incentives of the economy, requires that owners and managers treat labor as simply a "factor of production" to be maximally exploited. This leads to a detailed division of labor, driven by managers who, applying the principles of scientific management initiated by Frederick Taylor, peel away conceptual tasks from the labor process and distill jobs into simple tasks that are infinitely repeated. Managers think and conceive; workers, whose jobs require less and less skill, execute.[11]

The paradigmatic case of work stripped of almost all skill, utterly lacking in internal goods, is the assembly line, where work is fragmented into countless jobs, each including only a few basic tasks. The assembly line, described in one of Studs Terkel's interviews, is like an "endless serpent, all body and no tail . . . Repetition is such that if you think about the job itself, you slowly go out of your mind."[12] Yet workers do not become as simple or stupid as their work asks them to be; they "are not destroyed as human beings, but simply used in inhuman ways." Their "critical, intelligent, conceptual faculties, no matter how deadened or diminished," remain. Capitalism thus contains an enduring antagonism between what human beings are and what it asks and requires them to be, and the project of "adjusting workers to work . . . becomes a permanent feature of capitalist society."[13] Nothing short of a social revolution will reconcile the conflict, because reformist measures like democratic control of the workplace, or programs to improve worker morale will alter the incentives that drive profit and degrade the character of work. On this view, what Veblen called the "instinct of workmanship," or what Marx had earlier and more radically characterized as "freely conscious production"—the tendency of workers to take an interest in work in part for its own sake, to both discover and invest in it a sense of purpose—is fundamentally at odds with the organization of the modern economy.[14] The degradation of work is the price we pay for the affluence of the modern economy, regardless of whether that affluence is ours to share.

The problem with this blanket criticism of work under capitalism is not that it is wholly wrong. It is not, and under conditions of global trade the ravages of capitalism may become more visible with time. The problem is rather that the analysis casts the cause of our troubles too narrowly, and the cure too broadly. It is not simply capitalism but the nature of work that issues in a basic and recurring problem: the work society needs its members to do is not always (and perhaps is only rarely) aligned with the full powers we bear as human beings, or for that matter with the particular tendencies we possess as individuals. This tension is true not only for societies devoted to productivity but also for those devoted to piety, or self-defense, or personal liberty, or some mix of these and other goods. Social fit, or the alignment between individual talent and social need, and personal fit, the alignment between work and an individual's best purposes, are not easily satisfied simultaneously. A permanent resolution of this endemic conflict might arrive with the sort of social revolution Marx imagined, but even that would seem to require socializing our identities to the point where we cannot identify with personal goods that are inconsistent with social goods. The tension would remain, in a different form, even if a revolution inaugurated new relations of production.

If the problem is deeper than our particular mode of production, the solution may be more particular and more nuanced than wholesale revolution. Reformist measures, even though they may not immediately touch the incentives at the core of capitalism, nonetheless offer some hope for integrating the promise of the human personality and the process of work. One starting point for such measures lies in identifying the internal goods that work as we know it contains. Because internal goods are particular and specific to a given activity, we should hold off on a blanket condemnation of the modern world of work in favor of tending more carefully to particular kinds of work. Those on the outside—social critics, philosophers, observers, even customers—often know very little about the goods that particular kinds of work offer. There is little reason to assume that all work, or all work that is lacking the conventional signs of social status, is as degraded as the worst assembly-line jobs. Many jobs, such as selling cars or working in a supermarket, may possess important internal goods that only careful attention reveals. It is through acknowledging these goods that we come to understand what we can hope for from work, and only through understanding this can we know what a social revolution, were it to come, should achieve.

To better see how internal goods might be identified in a particular case, it is helpful to consider Anthony Kronman's argument about lawyering. While the law is a high-status career, status is no proxy for internal goods, and the legal profession today, Kronman argues, is afflicted by a "crisis of morale" that flows from having lost hold of the best goods the practice contains. These goods can be summarized in the idea of "practical wisdom," something that not only benefits lawyers in their professional role but also in a sense constitutes them—at least in the ideal—and contributes to a kind of fulfillment that is both personal and professional. The case method of legal education, combined with the activities of counseling and advocacy, requires practitioners to judge and advise on a range of problems and conflicts, and this in turn supports an intellectual habit of cool detachment, on one hand, and emotional capacity for sympathetic identification, on the other.[15] Combined, these qualities instill a kind of practical wisdom. They not only allow people to give good counsel but can also equip them to live happier lives more generally.

Practical wisdom, Kronman argues, allows people to look back at critical moments in their lives with that combination of sympathy and detachment that facilitates both integrity and self-understanding. Remembering ourselves as we were in the past is often painful, Kronman observes, because we are likely to have regret for what we might have been, had other choices been made, other paths followed. Such regret might be avoided with a steely habit of forgetting how we were in the past, but this comes at a cost of self-deception and even a measure of disintegration, for it demands that we separate ourselves in the present from ourselves in the past. Alternatively, the sort of practical wisdom that lawyering can instill facilitates an integrity that is not crimped. With it, Kronman says, one can face the past, "with its lost loves and abandoned dreams," with both understanding and empathy.[16]

This account of lawyering as a practice or a calling suggests how careful attention to both the experience of work and the standards internal to work can illuminate the internal goods that work conveys. Lawyering brings a certain status, perhaps. But one can attain status in many ways. A law practice provides a plentiful income, too, but it would be more effective to win the lottery. It is not status or income that renders law a fulfilling career, but rather the internal practical wisdom that comes from the activity itself.

Kronman also suggests how defending a particular account of internal goods (in this case, practical wisdom) depends on a broader conception of the moral world. Practical wisdom, on Kronman's argument, is a valuable possession in a moral world that presents us with decisions and options of a particular character. Specifically, individuals from time to time face grave questions that have no single and definitive answer. The gravity of such choices, perhaps involving career, marriage, or rival duties, is more weighty because the consequences are transformative and not perfectly reversible. In making them, we cannot continue to keep all our options open at all points into the future. These choices shape us, and do so somewhat irrevocably. Nor is there a single standard that can show one choice above all others as best. Inhabiting such a world, we cannot expect to possess a perfectly harmonious soul, unified around a single conception of the good. On the contrary, if some of our most important choices involve ends that are incommensurable, then some regret with respect to our past choices is an ever-present possibility. Regret is possible because even successful commitments require, at one point in time, foreclosing on other worthy projects and forgoing other worthwhile goods. Practical wisdom supports a good relation to ourselves, by accommodating regret without fueling it. It is a good not because it exercises what is highest or best in us, but because it facilitates a kind of integrity and happiness that is at home in this kind of moral world.

Kronman's account also shows how we might understand and judge internal goods even when we don't stand inside the practice that conveys them. This requires practitioners who engage in a certain kind of philosophy about activity, like Kronman. Yet at the same time there is a limit to how fully we can identify the internal goods that come through work without actually participating in those goods. The internal goods of lawyering cannot be tested or tried out, as we might test drive a new car. We cannot, when choosing a career, have complete and full information about the goods involved. Even when spokesmen like Kronman describe the internal goods of a practice, accepting a practice as a calling requires some trust in the judgment of those who have sustained the practice. This trust need not be blind, however. As Kronman's account of the practice of law shows us, some independent judgment is possible. The project of judgment is bottom-up: it starts with a particular activity and attends to the specific habits of mind and character that the work instills. Beyond this, any full account of internal goods needs to say something about how these habits of mind and character contribute to doing the job well, and also how they contribute more generally to living and faring well. In the case of lawyering, the combination of practical judgment and empathetic understanding—the internal goods Kronman specifies—contribute, as he argues, not only to being a lawyer but also more broadly to living a good life. They are qualities that assist us in the art of living. Other kinds of careers may contribute in other ways; and jobs, too, are likely to have their own distinctive internal goods.

It is difficult to identify the internal goods relevant to particular lines of work, and we should not be too quick to judge particular jobs or careers as simply lacking them. Internal goods may be hard to locate even at an individual level, with respect to one's own work. One source of the difficulty comes from the motivational force of external goods, which can crowd out an appreciation of internal goods and leave individuals less open to the importance of the inner rewards various activities may offer.[17] The difficulty of appreciating internal goods also derives from the way internal goods raise deep philosophical questions about the good life. They are good, after all, not only with respect to the activity that supplies them. Their goodness also consists in the way they contribute to a life well lived. By entertaining questions about the good life, the business of assessing and evaluating practices thus entails moral questions of the most pressing and difficult sort, questions for which there is likely no final answer. At the same time, these questions are in a sense inescapable: the ideal of fulfilling careers, so prominent in our culture, leads unavoidably to such questions. Practices and the internal goods they involve situate the larger quest for understanding the good. To participate in a practice also involves a leap of faith, or commitment. We take a chance, knowing that we cannot know all we need to know in advance of the commitment, with no other choice but to trust that the internal goods of the practice might carry with them some partial answer to larger questions about what is good.[18]

The Discipline of Fulfillment

The difficulty of finding our way with respect to questions about the good, as well as the element of trust that practices require, may in part account for the contemporary tendency to identify callings with passion, as if the fulfillment they bring is something easily won. Conflating the calling with one's passion avoids the difficult questions concerned with identifying and judging internal goods. Internal goods, by contrast, involve pleasure but are not about easygoing fulfillment. They depend more on self-restraint and commitment than on spontaneous passion or undisciplined self-expression. Internal goods require competence in an activity; they are not grasped straight away or in one's sleep but accrue as one's proficiency in an activity grows. The internal goods that come with sales or research would require being good at those activities. That in turn may demand sustained commitment. To realize the internal goods that come from a practice takes discipline; over time, as proficiency grows, the standards of the practice are no longer felt as constraints. Practices certainly facilitate some kind of self-expression, but they are formative before they are expressive. One has to learn the ropes before one climbs.

If born more of striving and persistence than of easy passion, still, internal goods promise an important kind of fulfillment. The fulfillment involved in practices is the hard-won consequence of training and dedication, of following constraints rather than shedding them for the sake of releasing inner passion. Although learning in a practice requires an amount of trust, proficiency in a practice requires less, and the most proficient express themselves not only through that practice but also by extending or even transforming it. The most outstanding poets, engineers, and athletes redefine what it means to be excellent in their respective practices. They do not so much violate the standards as they extend them. Because practices are not perfectly fixed, the most able can transform what it means to be proficient. Practices supply the situation for fulfilling self-expression.

The concept of a practice offers a way of grounding the promise of fulfillment. It also helps make sense of what it would mean to have an ideal fit with our work. To fit work in this sense is to have the abilities that equip us to share in the internal goods that work offers. Like the calling, work as a practice lends a deeper purpose to the exercise of our aptitudes than their function in the market can provide. Aptitudes are not simply the way we earn a living, nor are they strengths by which we triumph over others. Rather they are the means by which we come to possess the internal goods our work offers. But unlike either the Protestant calling or the exalted promise of fulfillment embraced by Friedan, internal goods bid us to carefully attend to the specific character of work. The Protestant doctrine of the calling endorsed diligent work in some "settled path," but one path was as appropriate as another, so long as it was not socially or individually damaging. Among the range of permissible callings, the Protestant ethic was indifferent. The Protestant doctrine of the calling emphasized diligence, persistence, devotion, and contribution in general, without offering any way of assessing how a particular sort of work might be good for a particular individual. Because it enjoined a generalized devotion to work, regardless of the work's character, it functioned as a moral tool that facilitated the exploitation of workers in the Industrial Age. Its residue today supports a lingering compulsion to work, regardless of what the work is for or where the profits go.

The idea of practices, however, is not so indiscriminate. In the end it asks something not only of us but also of work. Although many sorts of work will provide internal goods of some kind, it is not likely that all work will supply them equally well. The idea of a practice thus serves as a critical standard for work—far more, for instance, than does the Protestant calling. At the extreme, it points to a radically different kind of economy—one oriented as much to internal goods as economic ones. Yet even in the economy as we know it, the ideal of practices that carry internal goods can offer a critical point of orientation that guides both individual choices and larger efforts at reform. The organization of work is not something wholly fixed; there is room for shaping work in light of the internal goods it might bring. Where our efforts fail and work cannot supply much in the way of internal goods, there is far less reason for the devotion to work that characterizes a work ethic. In such cases, a strategic approach to work—where we work to secure external goods—would seem best.

And when work does supply worthwhile internal goods, still it will likely fall short of answering our every longing or potential. Internal goods are too specific and the discipline they require too narrow to suggest that we might ever be perfectly and wholly fitted to work. Human beings are too large and many-sided for that: even when it fits, work does not engage our whole self. Work may offer internal goods, and these might be the basis for a reasonable devotion to it. We may in our way come to love it. Yet it is in exactly such cases that work threatens to consume more than its share of our energy and spirit. A strategic approach to work is thus always part of work, even at its best: a healthy source of resistance to work's tendency (especially when it is fulfilling) to colonize other parts of life, it reminds us that even fitting work has its place.

Conclusion: The Place of Work

Practices offer the best way of understanding the promise of work: they show what it would mean to ideally fit our work, and they make sense of the sort of devotion to work characteristic of our work ethic. This promise, as we have seen, has animated powerful arguments for full inclusion in the world of work, such as those offered by John Stuart Mill and Betty Friedan. Practices answer this promise without simply asserting work's transcendent purpose, without imposing great purposes on work from the outside. Rather, the concept of a practice shows how purposes can be located within the process of the work itself. These purposes might seem narrow, since they adhere to conventions. The goods that come from chemistry or nursing, for example, do not show why they or the larger conventions that define chemistry or nursing are good. But participating in and reflecting on internal goods may lead one to consider broader moral standards that bear on conventions themselves. In this way, practices are the worldly point of contact with philosophic reflection. They both ground and invite deliberation concerning comprehensive questions about the good. They do not impose such conceptions on work; this is their advantage over the Protestant calling or the Millian model of fulfillment. By describing how the activity of work might be a source of fulfillment and occupy a central place in a life well lived, practices show what just work involves—where justice is not invoked in the narrow sense (paying one's debts, respecting rights) but in the larger sense of receiving what one ideally deserves.

Social Contribution

Yet this understanding of just work neglects a crucial component of justice: the common good. For his part, Alasdair MacIntyre thinks practices need to include a kind of service to the common good. He points not only to the sort of internal good we saw in the last chapter but also to a second sort of internal good, one from a social perspective that is more obvious and more important: the actual product of the practice, insofar as it can be produced only through the practice itself. So aside from the actual life a painter lives, the other internal good to the practice of painting is found in the paintings that are produced. Internal to law, we might say, are the actual arguments, or the cases won and lost; internal to farming, the crops. MacIntyre takes these to be internal because they are necessarily connected with a practice. While paintings stand external to the painter, they are internal to the practice in that they can be made only by the practice of painting. One can get status many ways, but the only way to produce a house is to engage in the practice of building.

Yet the products of practices are not internal in quite the same way as are the goods of character, for they do not exclusively accrue to those who participate in the practice. Architecture may be a practice, but the blueprint goes to the buyer. The portrait, the game, the dinner, the lesson all contribute something to those outside the practice of painting, baseball, cooking, or teaching. The products of practices affect the larger society, for better or for worse. For this reason practices are not entirely self-contained; their moral standing depends on their internal norms, standards, and rewards, and also on their effect on the larger society. Practices may be evil or good, and any full account of the justice of practices—indeed, of work as a practice—needs to evaluate the products of practices from a social perspective.

Only reluctantly does MacIntyre concede that practices might have vicious effects on the larger society. Because he focuses mainly on the way practices constitute a good life for those who participate in them, he tends to neglect the relation between internal goods and the common good. Robbing banks, for instance, might count as a practice. Bank theft could offer a range of internal goods—a certain clever habit of mind, control of the passions, decisiveness under stress, even a kind of courage. As a practice, bank theft would be more about the perfect theft than merely theft—as in the film *How to Steal a Million,* where the aim is not simply to steal successfully but to steal perfectly, with elegance and deftness.[1] Successful thievery requires rare technical skill as well as trust and loyalty among thieves. Bank theft could bring, then, not only riches and reputation but also internal goods: pursued in the "right" way, bank robbery could count as a practice. This example shows that work as a practice may be just in one respect yet not in another. It may give those who do it internal rewards, and by virtue of these develop their capacities. Yet from the perspective of the larger society or the common good, it may be woefully unjust. The fit that comes with internal goods does not offer a complete account of work's justice.

It is better to distinguish between what contributes to the common good and the internal goods that come to those who participate in practices. Practices may be rewarding for those who do them and yet be socially evil. Or to reverse the mix, activities may be useful socially yet fail to impart meaningful internal goods. They may not involve what MacIntyre calls "a certain sort of life" that is itself desirable—but they produce things that contribute to the needs and wants of others in society. Every society has need of things that are not intrinsically good to produce, and for that reason not every job will count as a practice. Indeed, in his discussion of intrinsically rewarding practices, most of MacIntyre's examples are not drawn from the world of work—he turns instead to the fine arts, science, and games. As for the disjunction between work and practices, MacIntyre asserts that "the kind of work done by the majority of people in the modern world cannot be understood in terms of the nature of a practice with goods internal to itself." He attributes this disjunction to the removal of production from the household, which detached the world of work from the community of households. In the modern world, MacIntyre says, work is not about sustaining communities but rather biological survival and "institutionalized acquisitiveness."[2]

The problem, as we have seen, is not the "modern world" (consider Aristotle's discussion of ancient slavery). The problem comes from the tension between what societies need and what individuals deserve. Societies in every age need certain things done that are not fulfilling to do. Social fit (the alignment of our aptitudes with the tasks society brings into being) and personal fit (what individuals need to develop their capacity and potential) are not easily reconciled. Work as a practice is a way of describing what it would mean to ideally fit our work—but it omits any consideration of social fit, and thus offers only a partial account of work's justice. Contemporary advocates of the calling are far too quick to assume that the "reappropriation of the idea of work as a calling" is consistent with "work as a contribution to all."[3] They fail to recognize any tension between work that contributes to the common good and work that is "intrinsically interesting and valuable"; but this is exactly the difficulty that "reappropriation" of the calling must face when it leaves out the Calvinist God. The Protestant calling did not depend on work's being interesting or rewarding, only on its being useful—and therefore pleasing to God. But we cannot so easily deduce the intrinsically worthwhile from the useful. A religion of work is no substitute for religion.

Improving Work

Stripped of the theological or simply optimistic assumptions that blanket all work with the promise of fulfillment, work is at best a partial good. Few jobs will fully satisfy the demands of practices, which is to say that work will often fall very short of the ideal fit to which the promise of work points. This, however, does not warrant rejecting "modern society" root and branch. There are different ways that we might address work, even when perfectly fitting work is unrealized. In the gap between bad fit and perfect fit is immense room for small improvements. We might address the conditions of work, for example, in creative and sensible ways that bring it closer to the ideal of a practice without undercutting its productivity. Even the most dismal work might be made better.

The classic assembly line, as we saw in Chapter 8, will always fall far short of offering fitting work. The jobs are repetitive and boring, physically arduous, and extremely dangerous. Yet they are, for many, some of the "last great jobs in America." In 1992 when Ford wanted to hire about 900 people for its Taurus assembly line in Atlanta, more than 7,000 people showed up to apply. But as Ford's training coordinator said, "They only see $18 an hour. They don't realize that what they've been hired for is the assembly line."[4] Whatever its wage, assembly-line work is still brutal. However, there is more than one way to structure a line. Some companies have experimented with alternatives, for the sake of organizing the work in a way that better fits individual capacities. Having groups of workers follow entire components through the production process, for example, can alleviate the worst aspects of assembly-line work and render it more suitable to human capacities and energies. Though these techniques can be productive, some argue that management rejects them nonetheless, because they too greatly empower workers.[5] Yet such efforts may make work that fits badly fit better.

While the process of the work itself may be restructured to better fit individuals, it is also possible that, holding the work process the same, the conditions and the context of a job might make the work, considered overall, fit better. Consider, taking an unusual case, the task of grape picking for raisin production. This is dirty, painful, and monotonous work, done by necessity on the knees and often in 100-degree heat. Picked by hand, the grapes must be laid on small trays beside the vines, where they dry in the sun for several weeks before they are rolled into balls, and, after further curing, carried from the fields to be boxed. The best pickers pick 300 to 400 trays of grapes a day; those who are merely industrious might pick 200. Victor Davis Hansen, who grew up on a raisin farm and worked it until it went bankrupt, calls it "the worst job in America, a vocation right out of the poet's inferno. Nothing—dusting vines in a fog of Dibrom toxicity, periodically climbing down into the century-old cesspool to shovel the grease off the sandy bottom, packing bearings inside a chemical spray tank, or trying to teach Euripides and Catullus each year to the distracted and illiterate at Fresno State— comes close," he says, to the harvesting of raisins.[6]

This description is alarming, and Hansen means to show the work as exactly the sort that does not fit well with human capacities but, rather, stunts and constrains the development of those capacities. Nevertheless Hansen laments the loss of his family farm—suggesting that the way we fit our work depends on not only the task itself but also its context. Picking grapes on one's own farm is one thing; it's another when you are a laborer hired for the task. On Hansen's account, the hired hands and the owners make about the same amount of money. But working *one's own* land transforms the task. To work for one's own extends the range of decisions and widens the responsibility that attends decisions. However, ownership is cherished by Hansen not because it conveys great authority or control—as he describes it, the farmer is quite powerless in the face of corporate buyers, supermarkets, banks, and weather. Rather, ownership offers the promise of handing something down (not just a financial asset but a way of life); it enlarges perspective by connecting work to a purpose larger than money. Situated in the context of sustaining a family, of passing on a way of life and reproducing a sort of character that itself emanates from the work, the separate tasks of farming—the planting, tying, spraying, picking—are subsumed in larger practices that can be linked more profoundly to human purposes. Ownership matters because of the way it situates discrete tasks in larger and worthwhile practices. This suggests, too, the importance of democratically organizing the workplace to generalize the benefits that come, on a smaller scale, through a sense of ownership.[7]

Sharing or rotating job roles is another possible way to deal with work that does not carry internal goods. Some bad work is necessary and useful, but insisting that only a few carry the burden of this work makes those workers the instruments of others. Michael Walzer, in his discussion of "hard work," recommends sharing, and contemplates a national service program akin to the corvée.[8] The sharing of bad work might be structured as a rotation, the way military service is sometimes allocated to all citizens for a year or two. But the sharing might also be, according to Walzer, *symbolic,* where citizens generally would take part in the worst tasks society makes necessary only occasionally—for a Saturday here or there. While such symbolic sharing would not prevent the necessity of having some individuals concentrate on the least desirable tasks, it would work to prevent the stigmatization of those individuals. It would express that society as a whole values not only the task but also those who perform it. There is a tendency to wish away the bad work we make necessary, and to turn away from those who do such jobs. To engage them as human beings is to risk recognizing the violence that the work—work necessary for our own convenience—does to the development of others. Sharing work, even in a symbolic way, helps guard against our tendency to render those who do the worst work socially invisible.

Take, for example, the chores involved in housework and homemaking. As we saw, Betty Friedan argued that the problem with housework was that it was beneath the capacities of human beings.[9] Friedan thought that nearly all housework was make-work, and that since much of it was simply unnecessary, it could be generally abandoned. However, most have not found the work associated with the household so dispensable. At the same time, many have discovered what the other part of Friedan's argument held true: paid work is often preferable to the unpaid work of the household.[10] Insofar as this is true for a couple, the best approach to housework may be analogous to what it might be for undesirable work in the larger society: share it. Sharing household work is one way of revaluing it (short of offering it a wage), of ensuring that the work is not invisible and unrecognized, and of distributing it justly.[11]

But sharing work might be easier in a household than in a larger society. Indeed, enforcing the sharing of work would likely require an impressive degree of coercive force. In addition, when it comes to many sorts of work it is simply impractical to share the burden. Were we to share the garbage collection, the care of the sick, the carting and storage of hazardous waste, the mining, the hauling and driving, we can be pretty sure that most of this work would not be done very well. Specialization does cause things to be done more finely. So when work fits human beings very badly, and when the options for abolishing or restructuring or sharing the work are exceedingly limited, there remains the possibility of *limiting* the work. As we saw in the discussion of domestic service, this is often the most crucial strategy for protecting the space in which meaningful purposes might be pursued outside of work.

In the 1930s, Kellogg's in Battle Creek, Michigan, instituted a six-hour day—a policy that persisted for some workers through the 1980s.[12] Although it began as a response to mass unemployment, it offered a "capitalist version of liberation to the modern world." For the first time, it appeared as if leisure—always the prerogative of the few (who exhorted others to work, of course, so their prerogative might be protected)—might characterize the condition of many. Yet even if "mass leisure" does not come to pass, some added leisure for those who carry the burden of work that fits us least would be an apt way of acknowledging that they, too, deserve a life that allows them to serve their own purpose.

Finally, we should not overlook the fact that even the most routine jobs have their claims. When work does not qualify as a practice in the ideal sense, it may yet carry internal goods—even if these come only in moments and glimpses. The ideal of a practice asks that we remain alive to these moments and not prematurely dismiss their possibility. It cautions us against accepting too complacently the view that work is all discipline.

Still, work is never without its discipline. The distance between the ideal of a practice and the lived experience of work suggests that work's discipline is what will be felt most keenly. It is through this discipline that work reveals our dignity. Work does not "give" dignity to our lives through the excellence or happiness it fosters.[13] The dignity of work comes less from its ideal promise than from the way we show, through it, a determination to endure what is difficult for the sake of discharging our responsibilities and contributing to society. It is less the source of our happiness than the illustration that we deserve happiness. Through work, we reveal our tough-minded commitment in the face of conditions that cannot bend exactly to our will. When this commitment brings a partial triumph over an unaccommodating world, work illuminates something of the dignity that resides in us independent of the character of our work. It expresses a kind of defiance, for we willfully ignore the ultimate resistance of a world we yet try to shape. Thus work reveals, though it cannot produce, the dignity of those who take their condition to be at least partly of their own making.[14]

Thinking through the ideal of fitting and fulfilling work—imagining what work would be like were it to give us all we deserve—should temper our expectations of it and better allow us to see it as worthy, but also as something partial. The promise of work, if undeniable, is also not so secure as work's moralists would presume. Seeing clearly where work falls short on its promise should at once inspire efforts to improve it and buttress practical efforts to limit its claims. The contemporary focus on work mandates should be tempered by an agenda that also focuses on the once-familiar goals of a shorter workweek, regulations on overtime, and flexible hours. Tempering the value of work also protects against the abuse of that value in the name of practices that are exploitative—an abuse to which the work ethic is particularly prone.[15] The ideal of fit points to work's promise and also exposes its partiality. While it unsettles premature complacency about the world of work as we happen to find it, it also shows us that just work is often a matter of keeping work in its place.

Notes ▪ Acknowledgments ▪ Index

Notes

Introduction

1. Marsha Sinetar, *Do What You Love, the Money Will Follow: Choosing Your Right Livelihood* (New York: Dell Publishing Co., 1989).
2. Robert Frost, "Two Tramps in the Mud," in *The Poetry of Robert Frost* (New York: Henry Holt and Co., 1979), 277.
3. Richard Sennett, *The Corrosion of Character: The Personal Consequences of Work in the New Capitalism* (New York: W. W. Norton, 1998).
4. Paul Simon, "American Tune," *There Goes Rhymin' Simon* (Warner Brothers, 1973).
5. Philip Fisher, *Still the New World: American Literature in a Culture of Creative Destruction* (Cambridge, Mass.: Harvard University Press, 1999).
6. Ludwig Wittgenstein, *Philosophical Investigations,* trans. G. E. M. Anscombe, 3rd ed. (New York: Macmillan, 1958), 32.
7. Judith Shklar, *American Citizenship* (Cambridge, Mass.: Harvard University Press, 1991), 68.
8. Aleksandr Isaevich Solzhenitsyn, *The Gulag Archipelago, 1918–1956,* trans. Thomas P. Whitney and Harry Willetts, abridged by Edward E. Ericson (London: Collins Harvill, 1986); John Bowe, "Nobodies: Does Slavery Exist in America?" *New Yorker,* April 21 and 28, 2003.
9. A. Bartlett Giamatti, *Take Time for Paradise: Americans and Their Games* (New York: Simon and Schuster, 1989), 20.

10. John Locke, *An Essay concerning Human Understanding,* ed. with foreword by Peter N. Nidditch (Oxford: Clarendon Press, 1975), book II, chap. XXI, 262.

11. The following discussion is informed by Bernard Williams, especially *Shame and Necessity* (Berkeley: University of California Press, 1993), 103–129.

12. Studs Terkel, *Working* (New York: Ballantine, 1972), xiii.

13. Ibid., xiii.

14. Genesis 1–3.

15. Wendell Berry, *The Gift of Good Land* (San Francisco: North Point Press, 1981).

16. Hannah Arendt, *The Human Condition* (Chicago: University of Chicago Press, 1958), 80 n. 3.

17. Robert Wuthnow, *Poor Richard's Principle* (Princeton: Princeton University Press, 1996), 96; 92–104 generally.

18. Max Weber, *The Protestant Ethic and the Spirit of Capitalism,* trans. Talcott Parsons (London: Routledge, 1992), 182.

1. Democracy and the Value of Work

1. Adam Smith, *An Inquiry into the Nature and Causes of the Wealth of Nations,* ed. R. H. Campbell and A. S. Skinner (Indianapolis: Liberty Classics, 1981), reprint of 1976 Oxford University Press edition, V (i) 782; I (i) 20; Abraham Lincoln, "Address to the Wisconsin State Agricultural Society," September 30, 1859, in *Speeches and Writings, 1859–65* (New York: Literary Classics, 1989), 98–99.

2. Karl Marx, *The German Ideology* (New York: Prometheus Books, 1998), 37.

3. John Rawls, *A Theory of Justice,* rev. ed. (Cambridge, Mass.: Harvard University Press, 1999), 229.

4. Karl Marx, "Economic and Philosophic Manuscripts of 1844," in *The Marx-Engels Reader,* ed. Robert C. Tucker (New York: W. W. Norton, 1978), 84; on the anti-utopian character of liberalism, see Isaiah Berlin, "The Decline of Utopian Ideals in the West," in *The Crooked Timber of Humanity* (New York: Alfred A. Knopf, 1991), 20–48; also Rawls, *A Theory of Justice,* 249: "A society in which all can achieve their complete good, or in which there are no conflicting demands and the wants of all fit together without coercion into a harmonious plan of activity, is a society in a certain sense beyond justice."

5. A few recent examples include Keith Grint, *The Sociology of Work* (Malden, Mass.: Blackwell Publishers, 1998); Robert Wuthnow, *Poor Richard's Principle* (Princeton: Princeton University Press, 1996); and Howard Gardner, Mihaly Csikszentmihalyi, and William Damon, *Good Work: When Excellence and Ethics Meet* (New York: Basic Books, 2001). Trenchant accounts of work by political theorists include, in a Marxist vein, Jon Elster, "Self-Realization in Work and Politics," in *Alternatives to Capitalism,* ed. Jon Elster and Karl Moene (Cambridge: Cambridge University Press, 1989), 127–158, and in the democratic socialist tradition, Richard Arneson, "Meaningful Work and Market Socialism," *Ethics* 97 (April 1987): 517–545; Joshua Cohen, *On Democracy: Toward a Transformation of American Society* (New York: Penguin, 1983); Ian Shapiro, *Democratic Justice* (New Haven: Yale University Press, 1999); and Michael Walzer, *Spheres of Justice* (New York: Basic Books, 1981), 165–183; also see Adina Schwartz, "Meaningful Work," *Ethics* 92 (July 1982): 634–646.

6. For an unusually broad and sensitive account that goes well beyond concerns of efficiency, see Joanne B. Ciulla, *The Working Life: The Promise and Betrayal of Modern Work* (Oxford: Oxford University Press, 2000).

7. Political freedom does not demand that every person be autonomous in the sense that each be the sole author of his or her life. A pious person who lives unreflectively by her family's faith may lack autonomy yet recognize her life as her own. Endorsing one's life (as one's own) is not the equivalent of choosing a life or living out a life-plan of one's own design. See Evan Charney, "Taking Pluralism Seriously," Ph.D. diss., Harvard University, 2000.

8. Phillippe Van Parijs, *Real Freedom for All,* (Oxford: Oxford University Press, 1995), 33, 95. Van Parijs argues that a guaranteed minimum income would also be the most effective way of securing Rawls's difference principle, which states that once equal basic liberties are secured, social and economic inequalities are justifiable only if they are attached to offices open to all and also benefit (perhaps maximally benefit) the least advantaged. For Rawls's difference principle, see *A Theory of Justice,* 52–81.

9. Jon Elster, *Solomonic Judgments* (Cambridge: Cambridge University Press, 1989), 215.

10. The ways in which a universal basic income might violate reciprocity are detailed in Stuart White, "Liberal Equality, Exploitation, and the

Case for an Unconditional Basic Income," *Political Studies* 45, no. 2 (1997): 317–319, 312–326 generally. White's case seems to survive Van Parijs's reply: "Reciprocity and the Justification of an Unconditional Basic Income: Reply to Stuart White," *Political Studies* 45 (1997): 327–330. Gijs Van Donselaar also carefully shows how a guaranteed income is parasitic, in "The Benefit of Another's Pains: Parasitism, Scarcity, and Basic Income," Ph.D. diss., University of Amsterdam, 1997, especially chap. 4. The way a universal basic income compromises reciprocity is also central to the argument in Amy Gutmann and Dennis Thompson, *Democracy and Disagreement* (Cambridge, Mass.: Harvard University Press, 1996), 279–282.

11. These examples come from Van Donselaar, "The Benefit of Another's Pains," 136–141, 166–179.

12. John Rawls, "The Priority of Right and Ideas of the Good," in *Collected Papers* (Cambridge, Mass.: Harvard University Press, 2000), 455 n. 7, and "Reply to Alexander and Musgrave," in ibid., 253.

13. Rawls, *A Theory of Justice*, 96, 301. Rawls is not addressing work per se but rather the general category of obligations that flow from participation in a system of just institutions.

14. Gutmann and Thompson, *Democracy and Disagreement*, 293; the authors make ample provision for those who are barred by disability of circumstance from participating in the working life; also, they do not limit their conception of work to paid jobs—unpaid labor in the household counts as doing one's part.

15. Ibid., *Democracy and Disagreement*, 280. For an argument against the legal enforcement of an obligation to work, see Lawrence Becker, "The Obligation to Work," *Ethics* 91 (October 1980): 35–49. The fact that democracy cannot be neutral with respect to economic productivity because welfarist policies depend on a society's wealth means neither that justice is only possible in wealthy societies nor that from an interest in justice we should pursue wealth without limit: "Beyond some point, it [great wealth] is more likely to be a positive hindrance, a meaningless distraction at best if not a temptation to indulgence and emptiness," Rawls, *A Theory of Justice*, 258.

16. Gutmann and Thompson, *Democracy and Disagreement*, 280; see generally 280–293.

17. Stuart White shows how a universal basic income might be reconciled with the exploitation objection, in "Fair Reciprocity and Basic In-

come," in *Real Libertarianism Assessed: Political Theory After Van Parijs,* ed. Andrew Reeve and Andrew Williams (New York: Palgrave Macmillan, 2003), 136–160.

18. See ibid., 148–149.

19. For the aristocratic affirmation of leisure, see Josef Pieper, *Leisure: The Basis of Culture* (New York: Pantheon Books, 1952), especially 46–55.

20. Richard Arneson, "Is Work Special? Justice and the Distribution of Employment," *American Political Science Review* 84, no. 4 (December 1990): 127–147.

21. Again, Arneson, Cohen, Walzer, and Schwartz are notable exceptions; see note 5.

22. Arneson, "Meaningful Work," 528–529, 533–537, 539: "The central issue is fairness to people with disparate preferences," 537.

23. Ronald Dworkin, "Liberalism," in *Taking Rights Seriously* (Cambridge, Mass.: Harvard University Press, 1985), 191.

24. Rawls, *Political Liberalism,* 213; 212–254 generally.

25. The stringent view is endorsed by Ronald Dworkin in "Can a Liberal State Support Art?" in *A Matter of Principle* (Cambridge, Mass.: Harvard University Press, 1985), 221–233; Rawls, too, argues that "the principles of justice do not permit subsidizing universities and institutes, or opera and theater, on the grounds that these institutions are intrinsically valuable, and that those who engage in them are to be supported even at some significant expense to others who do not receive compensatory benefits." Rawls does allow for "perfectionist" arguments that invoke regulative ideals in what he calls the exchange branch, which is a special legislative body that convenes only after a just distribution of income and wealth is in place, and which funds public goods that are permissible yet optional from the perspective of what justice requires. In this branch, voting on spending items is coupled with approval of the taxes and revenues needed to fund them in a manner that ensures no one is taxed to support public goods without his consent; see *A Theory of Justice,* 247–248, 291–292; for a dissenting view, see Thomas Nagel, *Equality and Partiality* (Oxford: Oxford University Press, 1991), 133–138.

26. I would also argue that regulative ideals are relevant at the constitutional level. Indeed they are essential to Rawls's process of arriving at basic principles of justice. They form one side of the equation in what

Rawls calls "reflective equilibrium," where we compare principles of justice generated from an impartial "original position" against our most confident intuitive judgments, such as the conviction that religious intolerance and slavery are unjust. These intuitive convictions, for many, are based on comprehensive moral and religious and philosophic conceptions. They come from a public culture rich in argumentation and struggle. As such, they stand on their own in reflective equilibrium—they do not derive from the principles of justice we arrive at in the original position, but serve as a test of those principles.

27. Rawls, *Political Liberalism,* 214–216; 213–254 generally.

28. John Rawls, "Public Reason Revisited," in *Collected Papers,* ed. Samuel Freeman (Cambridge, Mass.: Harvard University Press, 1999), 584, 592–594.

29. Joseph Raz, "Facing Up: A Reply," *Southern California Law Review* 62 (1989): 1231; for his argument against the "exclusion of ideals," also see Joseph Raz, *The Morality of Freedom* (Oxford: Oxford University Press, 1986), 134–162, and "Facing Up: A Reply," 1232–1235.

30. Joseph Chan, "Legitimacy, Unanimity, and Perfectionism," *Philosophy and Public Affairs* 29, no. 1 (2000): 5–42; see the discussion of perfectionist ideals concerning meaningful work at 18–19. For an argument on behalf of a "legislative point of view" that gets beyond "the opposition of neutrality and perfectionism," see Alex Tuckness, *Locke and the Legislative Point of View* (Princeton: Princeton University Press, 2002), 85–114.

31. On the importance of deliberation about moral ideals in "the land of middle democracy," see Amy Gutmann and Dennis Thompson, *Democracy and Disagreement* (Cambridge, Mass.: Harvard University Press, 1996), 12–13, 39–51, and Stephen Macedo, ed., *Deliberative Politics* (Oxford: Oxford University Press, 1999), 6–7.

32. Arneson, "Meaningful Work," 537. Also see Rawls, *A Theory of Justice,* 464, where he claims that a well-ordered society would eliminate the worst aspects of a division of labor, where some are "servilely dependent on others," and might even generate "meaningful work for all." Whether a well-ordered society of Rawls's description would solve the problem of meaningful work is discussed below in Chapter 4.

33. See Chapter 2 for a discussion of whether some individuals might be prone to reject work that fits.

34. In the period from 1989 to 1999, between 51 and 58 percent of respondents in a series of Gallup polls said they "get a sense of identity from their job." Between 40 and 47 percent said their job is "just what they do for a living." See "Work and Work Place" polls, under Gallup Poll Topics, at www.gallup.com.

2. Fitting Work in the Contemporary Economy

1. John Rawls, *A Theory of Justice,* rev. ed. (Cambridge, Mass.: Harvard University Press, 1999), 464.
2. Michael Walzer, *Spheres of Justice* (New York: Basic Books, 1982), 165–183.
3. For details, see Clair Brown, *American Standards of Living* (Cambridge: Blackwell Publishers, 1994), 1–18.
4. Robert Reich, *The Work of Nations* (New York: Vintage Books, 1991), 177–184, 225–242. In line with this change, the U.S. Department of Labor's occupational classification system was revised in the 1990s to include the increase in the 1980s and 1990s of managerial, professional, and technical jobs. See *Revising the Standard Occupational Classification System,* Report 929, June 1999 (Washington, D.C.: Department of Labor, Bureau of Labor Statistics), 4. As a percentage of all occupations, managerial and professional jobs increased from 23.3 percent in 1982 to 30.3 percent in 1999; compiled from Bureau of Labor Statistics data by Sarah Reber, Department of Economics, Harvard University.
5. Reich, *The Work of Nations,* 173–180.
6. Studs Terkel, *Working* (New York: Ballantine, 1972), 157–158, and 153–158 generally.
7. Martha Nussbaum, "Human Functioning and Social Justice: In Defense of Aristotelian Essentialism," *Political Theory* 20 (May 1992): 216.
8. Rawls does argue for a "duty of assistance" to "burdened peoples," but this is not as demanding as the difference principle applied internationally; see John Rawls, *The Law of Peoples* (Cambridge, Mass.: Harvard University Press, 1999), 106. Some have argued for the international scope of Rawls's principles, principally Charles R. Beitz and Thomas W. Pogge. See in particular Pogge, *Realizing Rawls* (Ithaca: Cornell University Press, 1989), 240–280; Pogge, "An Egalitarian Law

of Peoples," *Philosophy and Public Affairs* 23, no. 3 (Summer 1994): 195–224; Beitz, "Rawls' Law of Peoples," *Ethics* 110 (July 2000): 682–683, 688–694; and Beitz, "International Liberalism and Distributive Justice: A Survey of Recent Thought," *World Politics* 51, no. 2 (1999): 275–279.

9. Pranab Bardhan, "Some Up, Some Down," in *Can We Put an End to Sweatshops?* ed. Joshua Cohen and Joel Rogers (Boston: Beacon Press, 2001), 50.

10. Cohen and Rogers, eds., *Can We Put an End to Sweatshops?* xiv.

11. For a thoughtful approach to labor standards governing sweatshops, see Archon Fung, Dara O'Rourke, and Charles Sabel, "Realizing Labor Standards," Cohen and Rogers, eds., in *Can We Put an End to Sweatshops?* 3–42.

12. For example, see the "Downsizing of America," a seven-part series in the *New York Times,* March 3–9, 1996.

13. For an account of this change, see Peter Capelli, *The New Deal at Work* (Boston: Harvard Business School Press, 1999). Also Peter Capelli, et al., *Change at Work* (Oxford: Oxford University Press, 1997).

14. For instance, William H. Whyte, *The Organization Man* (New York: Simon and Schuster, 1956), or David Riesman, *The Lonely Crowd* (New Haven: Yale University Press, 1950).

15. Daniel B. Cornfield, "Shifts in Public Approval of Labor Unions in the United States, 1936–1999," *Guest Scholar Poll Review,* The Gallup Organization, Princeton, www.gallup.com; also see Richard B. Freeman and Joel Rogers, *What Workers Want* (Ithaca: Cornell University Press, 1999), 65–89.

16. See New York Times, *The Downsizing of America* (New York: Times Books, 1996) for an account of downsizing in the 1990s. Men were more vulnerable than women to downsizing in the 1990s: between 1983 and 1998, the job tenure for male workers declined; see "Median Years of Tenure with Current Employer," Bureau of Labor Statistics, Washington, D.C., at www.bls.gov. Also see "Job Tenure Declines among Men," The Editor's Desk, *Monthly Labor Review,* October 1998, Bureau of Labor Statistics, Washington, D.C. For evidence that most do not think it likely they will be laid off or lose their job, see the "Work and Work Place" polls in Gallup Poll Topics on the Gallup Poll Web site, www.gallup.com.

17. See this perception, for instance, in Po Bronson, *Nudist on the Late Shift and Other Stories of Silicon Valley* (New York: Broadway Books, 1999), xxvii.

18. Pierre Bourdieu, "Job Insecurity Is Everywhere Now," in *Acts of Resistance: Against the Tyranny of the Market* (New York: W. W. Norton, 1998), 81–93. For the effects of education on job security, Lawrence F. Katz and David H. Autor, "Changes in the Wage Structure and Earnings Inequality," in *Handbook of Labor Economics,* ed. Orley Ashenfelter and David Card, vol. 3 (New York: Elsevier Science Publishing Co., 1999), 1467, 1481.

19. Capelli, *The New Deal at Work,* 7, 37, 42; 1–68 generally.

20. Rosabeth Moss Kanter, *When Giants Learn to Dance: Mastering the Challenge of Strategy, Management, and Careers in the 1990's* (New York: Simon and Schuster, 1989), 229–266.

21. This is especially true for men. See Pamela J. Loprest, "Gender Differences in Wage Growth and Job Mobility," *AEA Papers and Proceedings* 82, no. 2 (May 1992): 526–532. Also see Robert H. Topel and Michael P. Ward, "Job Mobility and the Careers of Young Men," *Quarterly Journal of Economics* 107, no. 2 (May 1992): 439–479.

22. Mary-Ann Glendon, *A Nation under Lawyers* (Cambridge, Mass.: Harvard University Press, 1994), 25–29.

23. On the way oligopolistic corporations and high rates of unionization gave rise to such "steady times," in contrast to the contemporary economy, see Robert Reich, *The Future of Success* (New York: Alfred A. Knopf, 2001), 30–35, 93–107.

24. Michael Lewis, *The New New Thing: A Silicon Valley Story* (New York: W. W. Norton, 2000), 50–67.

25. Bronson, *Nudist on the Late Shift,* xxiii, xxxiv, 4, 211.

26. John Bowe, Marisa Bowe, and Sabin Streeter, eds., with Daron Murphy and Rose Kernochan, *Gig: Americans Talk about Their Jobs at the Turn of the Millennium* (New York: Crown Publishers, 2000), xi. Also see Bronson, *Nudist on the Late Shift,* xxiii. Contrast with Terkel, *Working.*

27. Bowe, Bowe, and Streeter, eds., *Gig,* 7, 411, 38.

28. For an account of the trials imposed by the need to be flexible, see Richard Sennett, *The Corrosion of Character: The Personal Consequences of Work in the New Capitalism* (New York: W. W. Norton, 1998).

29. Mihaly Csikszentmihalyi, *Flow: The Psychology of Optimal Experience* (New York: HarperCollins, 1991), 63.

30. Ibid., 152; see 143–163 generally.

31. Richard Burke, "'Work' and 'Play,'" *Ethics* 82, no. 1 (October 1971): 33–47. Work as absorbing play overlooks another commonality between work and play: like work, in play there is often victory or defeat at stake. Both have winners and losers. As one CEO said of his compensation, which in the year 2000 was $137 million, "The money is a way to keep score." See "Spend, Spend, Spend," *New Yorker,* February 17, 2003, 132. The ideal of absorbing play neglects this spirited aspect of work and play, or rather looks beyond winning itself to the qualities of mind and character that winning reflects.

32. Mihaly Csikszentmihalyi, *Finding Flow: The Psychology of Engagement with Everyday Life* (New York: Basic Books, 1997), 61.

33. Csikszentmihalyi, *Flow,* 159.

34. Barbara Sher, *I Could Do Anything If I Only Knew What It Was* (New York: Dell Publishing, 1994), 31.

35. Paul Tieger and Barbara Barron-Tieger, *Do What You Are* (New York: Little, Brown, 1992), 92.

36. Paul and Sarah Edwards, *Finding Your Perfect Work* (New York: Penguin Putnam, 1996), 96.

37. Csikszentmihalyi, *Flow,* 144.

38. Nicholas Love, *The Pathfinder: How to Choose or Change Your Career for a Lifetime of Satisfaction and Success* (New York: Simon and Schuster, 1998), 17.

39. Karl Marx, "The German Ideology," in *The Marx-Engels Reader* (New York: W. W. Norton, 1972), 160.

40. Bertrand Russell, *In Praise of Idleness and Other Essays* (New York: Simon and Schuster, 1935), 9–29. For an account of his ambivalent socialism, see Alan Ryan, *Bertrand Russell: A Political Life* (New York: Penguin Press, 1988), 81–83.

41. Max Weber, *The Protestant Ethic and the Spirit of Capitalism,* trans. Talcott Parsons, introduction by Anthony Giddens (London: Unwin, 1985), 182; Ted W. Engstrom and David J. Juroe, *The Work Trap* (Old Tapan, N.J.: Fleming H. Revell Co., 1979).

42. Jeremy Rifkin, *The End of Work* (New York: G. P. Putnam's Sons, 1996); Juliet Schor, *The Overworked American* (New York: Basic Books, 1991); Stanley Aronowitz and William DiFazio, *The Jobless*

Future: Sci-Tech and the Dogma of Work (Minneapolis: University of Minnesota Press, 1994).

43. See the contrast between Lawrence Mead's *The New Politics of Poverty: The Non-Working Poor in America* (New York: Basic Books, 1992), 62, and his *Beyond Entitlement: The Social Obligations of Citizenship* (New York: Free Press, 1986), 82. In the earlier work, Mead is more ready to see work as a social obligation that may not be good for those who do it: "Work, at least in low-wage jobs, no longer serves the individual's interest as clearly as it does society's." The obligatory and self-denying character of work is muted in the later work, which gives more emphasis to the psychic rewards that even low-wage work offers: "People without jobs . . . are psychologically much worse off than the employed."

44. William Julius Wilson, *When Work Disappears* (New York: Alfred A. Knopf, 1996), xix.

45. William J. Clinton, "Text of President Clinton's Announcement on Welfare Legislation," *New York Times,* August 1, 1996, A24. The full name of the bill was the Work Opportunity Reconciliation Act of 1996.

46. NBC News/*Wall Street Journal* Poll, July 29, 1995, conducted by Roper, Question ID USNBCWSJ.080495.R19.

47. Amy Gutmann and Dennis Thompson, *Democracy and Disagreement* (Cambridge, Mass.: Harvard University Press, 1996), 277–290.

48. In 1998, 93 percent of household heads between the ages of twenty-five and fifty-four and with a net worth greater than $2.5 million were working. Figures compiled by Sarah Reber from the Survey of Consumer Finances.

49. Since 1973 the General Social Survey has asked people, "If you were to get enough money to live as comfortably as you would like for the rest of your life, would you continue to work or stop working?" The range since 1973 of those who say they would continue to work is between 62 and 75 percent; in 1998, the most recent year for which I have data, 68 percent report that they would continue to work. Tabulated by Sarah Reber from the General Social Survey; see James A. Davis and Tom W. Smith, *General Social Survey, 1972–1998,* computer file (Chicago: National Opinion Research Center, 1999).

50. Labor force participation for men age fifty-five and older has declined from more than 70 percent in 1948 to just over 40 percent in 1998.

This is attributable to earlier retirement, both involuntary and chosen. Bureau of Labor Statistics, Washington, D.C.

51. Judith Shklar, *American Citizenship: The Quest for Inclusion* (Cambridge, Mass.: Harvard University Press, 1991), 63–101.

52. Charles Taylor, *Sources of the Self* (Cambridge, Mass.: Harvard University Press, 1989), 211–233; also Michael Walzer, *The Revolution of the Saints* (Cambridge, Mass.: Harvard University Press, 1965), 199–231.

53. Andrew Jackson, "A Political Testament," in *Social Theories of Jacksonian Democracy,* ed. Joseph L. Blau (New York: Bobbs-Merrill, 1954), 17; Shklar, *American Citizenship,* 73–76.

3. The Justice of Fit

1. Nancy Rosenblum, *Membership and Morals* (Princeton: Princeton University Press, 1998), 349–351. The term comes from Albert O. Hirschman, *Shifting Involvements: Private Interest and Public Action* (Princeton: Princeton University Press, 1982).

2. Plato, *The Republic,* trans. and notes by Allan Bloom (New York: Basic Books, 1991), 46 [370b]; see also 51 [374b–e], 111 [433a].

3. Ibid., 94 [415a].

4. Ibid., 97 [419a].

5. Friedrich A. Hayek, *The Constitution of Liberty* (Chicago: University of Chicago Press, 1960), 96–97.

6. Milton and Rose Friedman, *Free to Choose: A Personal Statement* (New York: Harcourt, Brace, Jovanovich, 1980), 135.

7. K. Davis and W. E. Moore, "Some Principles of Stratification," in *Class, Status, and Power,* ed. R. Bendix and S. Lipset (London: Routledge and Kegan Paul, 1967); also Talcott Parsons, *The Social System* (London: Routledge and Kegan Paul, 1951), 69–86, 386–439.

8. For the effect of windfall wages on the recruitment of talent, see Robert H. Frank and Philip J. Cook, *The Winner-Take-All Society* (New York: Penguin, 1995); for the challenge of creating enough low-skill work, see Richard B. Freeman and Peter Gottschalk, *Generating Jobs: How to Increase Demand for Less Skilled Workers* (New York: Russell Sage Foundation, 1998). The problem of supplying enough low-skill work is the inverse of the worry that characterized the 1970s, when the concern was that people were overeducated relative to the

demands of most work; see Richard Freeman, *The Overeducated American* (New York: Academic Press, 1976).

9. Pope Leo XIII, "Rerum Novarum: The Condition of Labor" (1891), in *Catholic Social Thought: The Documentary Heritage,* ed. David J. O'Brien and Thomas A. Shannon (Maryknoll: Orbis Books, 1992), 15, 31.

10. John Ryan, *A Living Wage* (New York: Macmillan, 1906), 85, 91–105.

11. For an argument in favor of living wage legislation today, see Robert Pollin and Stephanie Luce, *The Living Wage: Building a Fair Economy* (New York: New Press, 1998); for an assessment of the historical significance of the movement from 1870 to 1920, see Lawrence B. Glickman, *A Living Wage: American Workers and the Making of Consumer Society* (Ithaca: Cornell University Press, 1997).

12. Slavery was among the worst roles, but not necessarily the worst in every respect. In some ways, particularly by virtue of their attachment to a household, slaves could be better off than landless laborers; see M. I. Finley, *The Ancient Economy* (Berkeley: University of California Press, 1973), 66.

13. Aristotle, *The Politics,* trans. with introduction by Carnes Lord (Chicago: University of Chicago Press, 1984), Book VII, chap. 10, 213.

14. Bernard Williams, *Shame and Necessity* (Berkeley: University of California Press, 1993), 111–112.

15. Aristotle, *Politics,* Book III, chap. 5, 93.

16. Ibid., Book I, chap. 5, 41. On this point—the extent to which slaves share in virtue—Aristotle's analysis is tortured; they do not utterly lack reason, he says, but share in it. They are capable of greater virtue than mere obedience. See Book I, chaps. 5–7, 13. For an account of Aristotle's theory of natural slavery that claims Aristotle thought slaves to be deficient in spiritedness, or *thymos,* rather than in reason, see Russell Bentley, "Loving Freedom: Aristotle on Slavery and the Good Life," *Political Studies* 47 (March 1999): 100–113.

17. Aristotle, *Politics,* Book III, chap. 6, 95.

18. Ibid., Book I, chap. 5, 41.

19. Ibid., chap. 6, 41.

20. See for instance his criticism of the egalitarian reforms of Phaleas in ibid., Book II, chap. 7.

21. Bernard Mandeville, "An Essay on Charity and Charity-schools," *Fa-*

ble of the Bees, or Private Vices, Public Benefits, Part I (Indianapolis: Liberty Classics, 1988), 267, 302, 287.

22. Speech of March 4, 1858, *Congressional Globe,* 35 Congress, 1st sess., 962.

23. Charles Fourier, *The Utopian Vision of Charles Fourier: Selected Texts on Work, Love, and Attraction,* trans. Jonathan Beecher and Richard Bienvenu (Columbia: University of Missouri Press, 1983), 317.

24. Thomas Jefferson to Roger C. Weightman, June 24, 1826, in *The Portable Thomas Jefferson,* ed. Merrill D. Peterson (New York: Penguin, 1977), 585.

25. Aristotle, *Politics,* Book I, chap. 13, 54.

26. Martha Nussbaum, "Non-Relative Virtues: An Aristotelian Approach," *Midwest Studies in Philosophy* 13 (1988): 32–53, and "Human Functioning and Social Justice," *Political Theory* 20, no. 2 (May 1992): 202–246.

27. Nussbaum, "Human Functioning," 221–222, and 216–223 generally.

28. See Colonel Rainborough, "The Putney Debates," in *Puritanism and Liberty,* ed. A. S. P. Woodhouse (London: J. M. Dent and Sons, 1992), 53: "For really I think that the poorest he that is in England hath a life to live, as the greatest he; and therefore truly, sir, I think it's clear, that every man that is to live under a government ought first by his own consent to put himself under that government."

29. Joseph Raz, *The Morality of Freedom* (Oxford: Oxford University Press, 1986), 161, 400–429.

4. The Strains of Service

1. Living a life of one's own means that we each have an essential interest in living our life "from the inside, in accordance with our beliefs about what gives value to life." Such a conviction is at the heart of contemporary liberalism; see Will Kymlicka, *Liberalism, Community, and Culture* (Oxford: Clarendon Press, 1989), 13, 48.

2. Daniel E. Sutherland, *Americans and Their Servants: Domestic Service in the U.S. from 1800 to 1920* (Baton Rouge: Louisiana State University Press, 1981), 169; Glenna Matthews, *"Just a Housewife": The Rise and Fall of Domesticity in America* (New York: Oxford University Press, 1987), 97; for numbers of women in the occupation, see David Katzman, *Seven Days a Week: Women and Domestic Service in*

Industrializing America (New York: Oxford University Press, 1978), 282–283, Tables 1, A-2; for a thorough earlier account, see Lucy Maynard Salmon, *Domestic Service* (New York: Macmillan, 1901).

3. Salmon, *Domestic Service,* 4; Catharine E. Beecher and Harriet Beecher Stowe, *The American Woman's Home* (1869; Hartford, Conn.: Stowe-Day Foundation, 1991), 318.

4. Katzman, *Seven Days a Week,* 226.

5. On servant wages relative to wages in other occupations for women, see Sutherland, *Americans and Their Servants,* 109–114. On the persistent shortage of servants in the nineteenth century, see ibid., 15–25; Katzman, *Seven Days a Week,* 223–228; and Nancy F. Cott, *The Bonds of Womanhood* (New Haven: Yale University Press, 1977), 48–49.

6. Salmon, *Domestic Service,* 19–26.

7. Ibid., 45, 27.

8. Ibid., 22 n. 2.

9. Daniel T. Rodgers, *The Work Ethic in Industrial America* (Chicago: University of Chicago Press, 1974), 30–40.

10. Alexis de Tocqueville, *Democracy in America,* trans. George Lawrence, ed. J. P. Mayer (New York: Harper and Row, 1966), 577; see 572–580 generally.

11. Ibid., 574.

12. Ibid., 573–574.

13. Ibid., 575–577.

14. Ibid., 576, 577; also see Locke's use of the same analogy in his description of governmental authority both established and limited by contract: John Locke, *Two Treatises of Government,* ed. Peter Laslett (Cambridge: Cambridge University Press, 1960), 362 (paragraph 139).

15. Tocqueville, *Democracy in America,* 578, 579.

16. Sutherland, *Americans and Their Servants,* 30–34.

17. Katzman, *Seven Days a Week,* 169.

18. Sutherland, *Americans and Their Servants,* 29.

19. Katzman, *Seven Days a Week,* 10.

20. Ibid., 173.

21. Inez A. Godman, "Ten Weeks in a Kitchen," *The Independent* 53 (October 17, 1901): 2462.

22. Katzman, *Seven Days a Week,* 161.

23. Sutherland, *Americans and Their Servants,* 29.

24. Katzman, *Seven Days a Week,* 162.

25. Katzman reports that the average working day for live-in domestic servants in the nineteenth century was between eleven and twelve hours; *Seven Days a Week,* 113–114. While noting that servants' working hours varied by household, region, and staff size, Sutherland writes that even by 1917, "more than a few servants continued to work twelve to fourteen hours a day"; *Americans and Their Servants,* 98.

26. Katzman, *Seven Days a Week,* 113–114.

27. Ibid., 10.

28. Godman, "Ten Weeks in a Kitchen," 2462.

29. *Chronological Development of Labor Legislation for Women in the United States,* ed. Florence P. Smith (Washington, D.C.: Government Printing Office, 1929); Katzman, *Seven Days a Week,* 111–112.

30. Edward Cadbury, M. Cecile Matheson, and George Shann, *Women's Work and Wages: A Phase of Life in an Industrial City* (London: T. Fischer Unwin, 1906).

31. Katzman, *Seven Days a Week,* 12.

32. Ibid., 11.

33. Ibid., 238.

34. James Fenimore Cooper, *The American Democrat,* introduction by H. L. Mencken (1838; Indianapolis: The Liberty Fund, 1981; repr. of 1931 Knopf ed., New York), 152.

35. See Alasdair MacIntyre, *After Virtue: A Study in Moral Theory* (Notre Dame: University of Notre Dame Press, 1984), 190–191.

36. Karl Marx, "Economic and Philosophical Manuscripts of 1844," *The Marx-Engels Reader,* ed. Robert C. Tucker, 2nd ed. (New York: W. W. Norton, 1972), 74.

37. Katzman, *Seven Days a Week,* 240.

38. Colonel Rainborough, "The Putney Debates," in *Puritanism and Liberty,* ed. A. S. P. Woodhouse (London: J. M. Dent and Sons, 1992), 53.

39. Edward Bellamy, *Looking Backward, 2000–1887* (Boston: Houghton, Mifflin, 1890), 68, 118–119.

40. Harriet Beecher Stowe, "The Lady Who Does Her Own Work," *Household Papers: The Writings of Harriet Beecher Stowe* (Boston: Houghton, Mifflin, 1896), 95; see 85–101.

41. Matthews, *"Just a Housewife,"* 97.

42. Christopher Lasch, *Haven in a Heartless World: The Family Besieged* (New York: Basic Books, 1979).

43. Beecher and Beecher Stowe, *The American Woman's Home*, 322–323, 324; on "the Care of Servants," see 302–334.

44. Sutherland, *Americans and Their Servants*, 165–169.

45. See, for instance, Michael Walzer on "hard work," in *Spheres of Justice: A Defense of Pluralism and Equality* (New York: Basic Books, 1983), 165–183.

46. In 1979 only 2.6 percent of employed women were domestic servants; by contrast, in 1940 the figure was 20.4 percent. The occupation has declined since its high in 1870, when 52.3 percent of employed women (numbering 960,000) worked in domestic service. Figures from *U.S.: A Statistical Portrait of the American People,* ed. Andrew Hacker, with Lorrie Millman (New York: Viking Penguin, 1981), 132–133.

47. Shellee Colen, "Housekeeping for the Green Card," *At Work in Homes: Household Workers in World Perspective* (Washington, D.C.: American Anthropological Association, 1990), 89–118.

48. Arlie Russell Hochschild, *The Time Bind* (New York: Metropolitan Books, 1997), and Hochschild, "The Nanny-Chain," *American Prospect* 11, no. 4 (January 2000), available at www.americanprospect .org.

49. Kymlicka, *Liberalism, Community, and Culture,* 48.

5. The Work Ethic and Callings

1. William A. Galston, *Liberal Purposes: Goods, Virtues, and Diversity in the Liberal State* (Cambridge: Cambridge University Press, 1991), 223.

2. Judith Shklar, *American Citizenship: The Quest for Inclusion* (Cambridge, Mass.: Harvard University Press, 1991), 68.

3. Alexis de Tocqueville, *Democracy in America,* trans. George Lawrence, ed. J. P. Mayer (New York: Harper and Row, 1966), 198.

4. Also see Seymour Martin Lipset, "The Work Ethic—Then and Now," *Public Interest* 98 (Winter 1990): 61–69; George J. Church, "The Work Ethic Lives," *Time* 130 (September 7, 1987): 40–43; Juliet Schor, *The Overworked American: The Unexpected Decline of Leisure* (New York: Basic Books, 1991), 17–42; for a dissenting view, see Robert J. Samuelson, "Overworked Americans?" *Newsweek* 119 (March 16, 1992): 50.

5. Raymond A. Katzell, "Changing Attitudes toward Work," in *Work in America: The Decade Ahead,* ed. Clark Kerr and Jerome M. Rosow (New York: Van Nostrand Reinhold, 1979), 45. Also see *The Gallup Poll: Public Opinion, 1994* (Wilmington, Del.: Scholarly Resources, 1995), 224.

6. Richard G. Braungart and Margaret M. Braungart, "Today's Youth, Tomorrow's Citizens," *Public Perspective* (Roper Center for Public Opinion) 6, no. 5 (August–September 1995): 4.

7. See, for instance, Robert Eisenberger, *Blue Monday: The Loss of the Work Ethic in America* (New York: Paragon House, 1989).

8. Roper Center at the University of Connecticut, *Public Opinion Online,* accession no. 0167559, question 31; accession no. 0167550, question 22.

9. Lawrence Mead, *The New Politics of Poverty: The Nonworking Poor in America* (New York: Basic Books, 1991), 61–63.

10. Lawrence Mead, *Beyond Entitlement: The Social Obligations of Citizenship* (New York: Free Press, 1986), 81–82.

11. Christopher Lasch, *The Culture of Narcissism: American Life in an Age of Diminished Expectations* (New York: W. W. Norton, 1978), 52–53.

12. Ibid., 53.

13. Ibid., 59, 68–69.

14. Daniel Bell, *The Cultural Contradictions of Capitalism* (New York: Basic Books, 1976), 21–25, 54–74, esp. 75.

15. Max Weber, *The Protestant Ethic and the Spirit of Capitalism,* trans. Talcott Parsons, intro. Anthony Giddens (London: Unwin Hyman, 1985), 44, 53.

16. Ibid., 60.

17. Ibid., 70, 71.

18. Ibid., 104, 111, 112; 101–128 generally.

19. Ibid., 117.

20. On the "affirmation of ordinary life," see Charles Taylor, *Sources of the Self: The Making of the Modern Identity* (Cambridge, Mass.: Harvard University Press, 1989), 211–247.

21. Edmund S. Morgan, "William Perkins on Callings," in *Puritan Political Ideas, 1558–1794,* ed. Morgan (New York: Bobbs-Merrill, 1965).

22. Ibid., 39.

23. Ibid., 53, 47.

24. On the relation of callings and order, and the associated importance

of the "settled courses," see Michael Walzer, *The Revolution of the Saints: A Study in the Origins of Radical Politics* (Cambridge, Mass.: Harvard University Press, 1965), 215–219.

25. Adrian Furnham and Maria Rose, "Alternative Ethics: The Relationship between the Wealth, Welfare, Work, and Leisure Ethic," *Human Relations* 40, no. 9 (1987): 561–574.

26. Weber, *Protestant Ethic*, 162.

27. See Robert H. Frank and Philip J. Cook, *The Winner-Take-All Society* (New York: Free Press, 1995).

28. Weber, *Protestant Ethic*, 182.

29. Ibid., 181.

30. Laura Pederson-Pietersen, "Callings," *New York Times*, September 19, 1999, B11; the column, which profiled "people whose work is their passion," appeared every third Sunday between October 1998 and April 2000. Also see Martha Finney, *Find Your Calling, Love Your Life* (New York: Simon and Schuster, 1998).

31. *The Shorter Oxford English Dictionary* (Oxford: Clarendon Press, 1993), I, 338–339, 1449; Robert Bellah et al., *Habits of the Heart: Individualism and Commitment in American Life* (Berkeley: University of California Press, 1985), 65–69; Richard Sennett, *The Corrosion of Character* (New York: W. W. Norton, 1999), 9, 120.

6. The Promise of Fulfillment

1. John Stuart Mill, *Principles of Political Economy, Books IV and V*, ed. Donald Winch (London: Penguin, 1970), 120.

2. Jeremy Bentham, *An Introduction to the Principles of Morals and Legislation* (Oxford: Clarendon Press, 1970), 39.

3. John Stuart Mill, *Autobiography* (New York: Signet Classics, 1964), 113.

4. John Stuart Mill, *On Liberty* (Cambridge: Cambridge University Press, 1989), 14.

5. Mill, *Autobiography*, 129.

6. Mill, *Principles of Political Economy*, 133; see Book IV, chap. 7 generally.

7. John Stuart Mill, "Subjection of Women," in *Essays on Sex Equality*, ed. with introductory essay by Alice S. Rossi (Chicago: University of Chicago Press, 1970), 241.

8. Ibid., 142, 143.

9. Mill, *On Liberty,* 59.

10. John Stuart Mill, "Nature," *Essays on Ethics, Religion, and Society,* in *Collected Works,* vol. 10 (Toronto: University of Toronto Press, 1969), 377–378, 375, 379.

11. Ibid., 381.

12. Ibid., 385.

13. Ibid., 395, see 393–395 generally; 399.

14. Mill, "Subjection of Women," 136–137.

15. Ibid., 151, 152, 141.

16. Ibid., 155.

17. Ibid., 165, 235, 233.

18. Ibid., 239, 241, 236.

19. Ibid., 179, 178. Mill's endorsement of traditional domestic roles within marriage "places serious limitations on the extent to which he can apply the principles of freedom and equality to married women," argues Susan Okin; see *Women in Western Political Thought* (Princeton: Princeton University Press, 1992), 227–230.

20. Mill, *Principles of Political Economy,* 314, 318–321; see generally Book V, chap. 11, "Of the Grounds and Limits of the Laisser-faire or Non-Interference Principle," 304–346.

21. See in this context Mill's highly qualified support for the state aid to the poor, in ibid., 333–336.

22. Mill, "Nature," 391.

23. Mill, "Subjection of Women," 147.

24. Mill, "Nature," 398; see *On Liberty,* chap. 3, 81: "The power of compelling others into it [following his way] is not only inconsistent with the freedom and development of all the rest, but corrupting to the strong man himself." On family as the nursery of the vices, see "Subjection of Women," 136, 163–166, 174–176, 213, 219–220.

25. Mill, "Subjection of Women," 236.

26. John Stuart Mill, *Utilitarianism* (Indianapolis: Hackett, 1979), 13, 8; 8–11.

27. Ibid., 8, 11, 10.

28. Mill, *On Liberty,* 62.

29. Ibid., 61.

30. Mill, "Nature," 393.

31. Mill, *On Liberty,* 52, 73, 51, 59, 15, 65, 67.

32. Ibid., 49.

33. Ibid., 60. On the idea that we each are prone to see only one side of the truth, see Mill's essay "Bentham," where he argues that "every circumstance which gives a character to the life of a human being, carries with it its peculiar biases; its peculiar facilities for perceiving some things, and for missing or forgetting others"; of Bentham's one-sided understanding Mill says, "For our own part, we have a large tolerance for one-eyed men, provided their one eye is a penetrating one: if they saw more, they probably would not see so keenly"; *Collected Works: Essays on Ethics, Religion, and Society,* vol. 10, ed. J. M. Robson (Toronto: University of Toronto Press, 1969), 91, 94.
34. Mill, "Subjection of Women," 194, 189.
35. Mill, *On Liberty,* 64.

7. Friedan's Careerism

1. Betty Friedan, *The Feminine Mystique* (New York: Bantam Doubleday Dell, 1984), originally published in 1963; introduction and epilogue added in 1973; additional essay "Thoughts on Becoming a Grandmother," included in 1983.
2. Ibid., 37.
3. Ibid., 248–249. Juliet Schor explains that hours of household labor remain constant after the introduction of labor-saving appliances as a result of "a distortion in the value of women's time," due to the fact that housewives are not paid. See Juliet Schor, *The Overworked American* (New York: Basic Books, 1991), chap. 4, "Overwork in the Household," especially 97.
4. Friedan, *Feminine Mystique,* 67, 133, 255, 256.
5. Ibid., 180, 314, 242, 15–32.
6. Ibid., 260, generally 258–262; 208.
7. Ibid., 67, 227, 255, 76–77, 174.
8. Sheila M. Rothman, *Woman's Proper Place: A History of Changing Ideals and Practices, 1870 to the Present* (New York: Basic Books, 1978), 97–132; for an earlier statement about the dangers of maternal overprotection, see Geraldine Youcha, *Minding the Children: Child Care in America from Colonial Times to the Present* (New York: Scribner, 1995), 260–262.
9. Friedan, *Feminine Mystique,* 304.
10. Ibid., 315, 313.

11. Ibid., 336.

12. John Stuart Mill, "Subjection of Women," in *Essays on Sex Equality,* ed. Alice S. Rossi (Chicago: University of Chicago Press, 1970), 179.

13. Friedan, *Feminine Mystique,* 334–335, 333.

14. Later Friedan retreated from the implication of her earlier writing, that motherhood as a vocation is not worthy of being chosen by capable women. See the 1983 afterword to *The Feminine Mystique,* "Thoughts on Becoming a Grandmother," 397–415.

15. Friedan, *Feminine Mystique,* 369.

16. Daniel Horowitz, *Betty Friedan and the Making of the Feminine Mystique: The American Left, the Cold War, and Modern Feminism* (Amherst: University of Massachusetts Press, 1998), 208–213.

17. C. Wright Mills, *White Collar: The American Middle Classes* (Oxford: Oxford University Press, 1951), 228.

18. William H. Whyte, Jr., *The Organization Man* (New York: Simon and Schuster, 1956), 137, 142.

19. Ibid., 152.

20. David Riesman, in collaboration with Reuel Denney and Nathan Glazer, *The Lonely Crowd: A Study of the Changing American Character* (New Haven: Yale University Press, 1950), 146; see generally 13–26, 136–146.

21. Ibid., 325, 326, 318, 330–334.

22. Daniel Bell, *The End of Ideology: On the Exhaustion of Political Ideas in the Fifties* (Glencoe, Ill.: Free Press, 1960), 261; see generally 222–262.

23. Ibid., 253.

24. See Harry Braverman, *Labor and Monopoly Capital: The Degradation of Work in the Twentieth Century* (New York: Monthly Review Press, 1998), 79; James Bernard Murphy in *The Moral Economy of Labor* (New Haven: Yale University Press, 1993) also describes self-realization through work not in expressivist terms of perfect fulfillment but in ways that emphasize the importance of combining conception with execution.

25. In the 1970s and 1980s, Friedan generally "tried to align herself with centrist American politics" and to obscure the radical commitments of the 1940s that informed so much of *The Feminine Mystique,* according to Horowitz, *Betty Friedan,* 235.

26. Friedan, "Epilogue," in *Feminine Mystique,* 385.

27. Elizabeth Anderson makes this argument about "modes of valuation" in her case against surrogate motherhood contracts. Anderson contends that surrogacy contracts, by introducing monetary payment for the labor of bearing children, "commodifies both women's labor and children in ways that undermine the autonomy and dignity of women and the love parents owe to children." See *Value in Ethics and Economics* (Cambridge, Mass.: Harvard University Press, 1993), 5, 8–11, 168; 168–189 generally.

28. Friedan, *Feminine Mystique*, "Thoughts on Becoming a Grandmother" [1983], 409.

29. Mill, "Subjection of Women," 142.

8. Work as a Practice

1. Robert Bellah et al., *Habits of the Heart: Individualism and Commitment in American Life* (Berkeley: University of California Press, 1985).

2. Ibid., 3–8, 70–71, 288.

3. Ibid., 66.

4. Ibid., 66, 69.

5. See Alasdair MacIntyre's discussion in *After Virtue: A Study in Moral Theory* (Notre Dame: University of Notre Dame Press, 1984), 187–191. Although MacIntyre discusses practices for the sake of elucidating the virtues rather than work, he does relate certain sorts of work to practices, and his description of a practice is at the core of the secular concept of callings that Bellah and colleagues advance. It is unclear whether MacIntyre means to imply that devotion to the excellence and goods particular to specific practices extends the capacity to achieve and conceive of a generic human excellence, or—more modestly—extends the conception of excellence and of the goods characteristic only of that particular activity; see *After Virtue*, 187.

6. For an account of the complexity that work in fast-food restaurants involves, see Katherine S. Newman, *No Shame in My Game* (New York: Vintage Books, 1999), 141–144.

7. Bellah et al., *Habits of the Heart*, 69.

8. MacIntyre, *After Virtue*, 188.

9. Ibid., 190.

10. MacIntyre says that playing tic-tac-toe, throwing a football, bricklay-

ing, and planting turnips are *not* practices, while football, chess, architecture, farming, physics, chemistry, biology, and creating and sustaining households *are* (see *After Virtue*, 187–188). It seems that building (as opposed to the profession of architecture) and gardening (which might include planting turnips) could also be practices. Since many simple activities can be situated as parts of more complex activities, the distinction relies on whether an activity offers the possibility of realizing internal goods.

11. Harry Braverman, *Labor and Monopoly Capital: The Degradation of Work in the Twentieth Century* (New York: Monthly Review Press, 1998), 51, 79, 96.

12. Studs Terkel, *Working* (New York: Ballantine, 1972), 222.

13. Braverman, *Labor and Monopoly Capital*, 96.

14. Thorstein Veblen, *The Instinct of Workmanship and the Irksomeness of Labor: Essays in Our Changing Order* (New Brunswick: Transaction Publishers, 1998), 78–96, and *The Instinct of Workmanship* (New Brunswick: Transaction Publishers, 1990).

15. Anthony Kronman, *The Lost Lawyer* (Cambridge, Mass.: Harvard University Press, 1993), 2, 109–162.

16. Kronman, *The Lost Lawyer*, 86.

17. Robert E. Lane, *The Market Experience*, (New York: Cambridge University Press, 1991), 371–372. Lane relates evidence suggesting that introducing payment (an extrinsic reward) for intrinsically interesting tasks reduces the enjoyment and interest individuals take in the task. Lane's concept of internal rewards, though distinct from MacIntyre's, gives empirical support to the general idea that extrinsic rewards crowd out an appreciation of internal goods. But the effect runs in both directions—the availability of intrinsic rewards also diminishes the importance of external rewards; see 391.

18. The dispositions cultivated by practices, MacIntyre says, also assist us in a quest for understanding the good more broadly. The enlarging and extending of our understanding of the good seems to be the ultimate end of practices for MacIntyre (see *After Virtue*, 187, 219). But this suggests that internal goods are more intellectual than need be the case. The dispositions inculcated by baseball, chess, farming, or medicine, for instance, do not necessarily lead to a deeper understanding of the good, although identifying and describing those internal goods does engage one (eventually) in profound moral questions about the

good. I agree with MacIntyre that any practice in "good order" involves some understanding of (and argument about) the internal goods involved in the practice (222), but it is perfectly possible to participate in a practice without developing a fully articulate intellectual understanding of the relevant internal goods. Judging, describing, and developing an intellectual understanding of internal goods is distinct from participating in activities that contain internal goods. Practices do situate a quest for understanding human goods, and they may even be a necessary starting point in developing such an understanding, but they need not produce such an understanding in all participants.

Conclusion

1. *How to Steal a Million* (like *The Thomas Crown Affair*) is about art theft rather than bank robbery.
2. Alasdair MacIntyre, *After Virtue: A Study in Moral Theory* (Notre Dame: University of Notre Dame Press, 1984), 227–228.
3. Robert Bellah et al., *Habits of the Heart: Individualism and Commitment in American Life* (Berkeley: University of California Press, 1985), 287–288.
4. Mary Walton, *Car: A Drama of the American Workplace* (New York: W. W. Norton, 1997), 285.
5. Stephen Marglin, "What Do Bosses Do?" in *The Division of Labour: The Labour Process and Class-Struggle in Modern Capitalism,* ed. André Gorz (Atlantic Highlands, N.J.: Humanities Press, 1976).
6. Victor Davis Hansen, *Fields without Dreams: Defending the Agrarian Idea* (New York: Simon and Schuster, 1996), 38–39.
7. Ian Shapiro, *Democratic Justice* (New Haven: Yale University Press, 1999), 161–179.
8. Michael Walzer, *Spheres of Justice* (New York: Basic Books, 1982), 184–196.
9. Betty Friedan, *The Feminine Mystique* (New York: Bantam Doubleday Dell, 1984), 67, 133, 255–256.
10. Arlie Hochschild, *The Time Bind* (New York: Henry Holt, 1997).
11. Also see Susan Moller Okin, *Justice, Gender, and the Family* (New York: Basic Books, 1989), 17–22.
12. Benjamin Hunnicutt, *Kellogg's Six-Hour Day* (Philadelphia: Temple University Press, 1996).

13. "Text of President Clinton's Announcement on Welfare Legislation," *New York Times*, August 1, 1996, A24.

14. Richard Sennett and Jonathan Cobb, *The Hidden Injuries of Class* (New York: W. W. Norton, 1972), 191–219.

15. Consider, for instance, Joseph Chamberlain's defense of British imperialism in Africa: "I think it is a good thing for him [the native African] to be industrious; and by every means in our power we must teach him to work . . . In the interests of the natives all over Africa, we have to teach them to work." See Roger Casement, "The Congo Report (1903)," in *Imperialism and Orientalism*, ed. Barbara Harlow and Mia Carter (Malden, Mass.: Blackwell Publishers, 1999), 322.

Acknowledgments

I am embarrassed that this book took all the help my friends could offer. But I am thankful that I have so many to thank. The outside readers for Harvard University Press gave much of themselves to the task, and their suggestions large and small were of crucial assistance. Michael Aronson at Harvard University Press was full of good ideas and steady encouragement. A number of generous colleagues read different versions of the manuscript, including Timothy Burns, Yannis Evrigenis, Samuel Fleischacker, Bryan Garsten, Sally Gibbons, Gary Jacobsohn, Marci Kanstaroom, James Nolan, Sarah Reber, Nancy Rosenblum, Andy Sabl, Timothy Shah, Shannon Stimson, Dennis Thompson, and Alan Wolfe. I have not done their patient and probing criticism justice, but it was nonetheless a great help. Richard Tuck's fruitful and offbeat comments were an education in themselves. I am grateful for Harvey Mansfield's gentle and warm advice. That several friends—Sam Beer, Istvan Hont, Pratap Mehta, and Glyn Morgan—immediately grasped the underlying motive to think through the problem of work was itself an immense encouragement, and their suggestions were impossible to forget. Margaret Muirhead cured many unhappy expressions in the text; I am thankful for her good cheer and good sense. I benefited from many spirited discussions with Peter Berkowitz, who put no bounds on his help. Michael Sandel, who was there at the beginning and an inspiration throughout, was steadfast in his support to the end. Finally, I am thankful for my parents' unqualified affection, which made this and much else possible.

Index

CPSIA information can be obtained
at www.ICGtesting.com
Printed in the USA
LVHW040459240223
740251LV00003B/387